Rainbow Edition

[handwritten] Placement tests
p 53
Scope + Sequence
p48-49

p22 mastery V

p26 mastery VI

Reading Mastery
Series Guide

Steve Osborn

S R A

Macmillan/McGraw-Hill
Columbus, Ohio

Contents

Masters of the Reading Arts

Masters of the Reading Arts! Students who can decode and comprehend; who apply thinking skills and background knowledge; who love literature and language — these are Masters of the Reading Arts. It's a challenging and advanced degree, but those who enroll in SRA's *Reading Mastery* can earn it with ease.

Reading Mastery is a complete basal reading program intended for students in the first through sixth grades. A few simple principles have guided the program since its inception in the 1960's, and they have played a large part in its resounding success.

- Along with the teacher, the program accepts complete responsibility for teaching every student how to read.
- All instruction is direct and unambiguous; tasks and activities are specified in detail.
- Every reading skill and strategy that students need is specifically taught, applied, and reviewed.
- Students receive consistent daily practice in reading, writing, listening, and speaking.
- Assessment is continuous; errors are corrected the instant they occur.

Decoding and Comprehension

There's no longer any doubt that phonics is the best method for teaching students how to decode, and *Reading Mastery* has always included phonics as an integral part of its instructional plan. But phonics is just the start. The real measure of a reading program lies in its ability to teach comprehension. In *Reading Mastery,* comprehension is specifically taught — not just tested — from the very first lesson. Students in *Reading Mastery* learn how to answer questions and how to make stories come alive. They learn the meanings of words and the forms of sentences. They draw story pictures and follow written instructions. They soon learn — through these and other techniques — how to comprehend the texts they decode.

Thinking Skills and Strategies

Reading Mastery places particular emphasis on the teaching of thinking skills and the acquisition of background knowledge. Specific step-by-step activities teach students not only how to infer, predict, and conclude, but also how to apply those skills to comprehension. No skill is taught for its own sake; every skill leads to reading.

No amount of skill development, however, can make up for a lack of background knowledge. That's why *Reading Mastery* includes realistic stories and factual articles that give students a broad and coherent view of the world they live in. Students learn important facts about physics, geography, astronomy, history, and other subject areas. These facts provide students with knowledge that they can apply to all their reading.

Literature and Language

A love of literature and language grows throughout *Reading Mastery.* It reaches its full flower when students read some of the world's greatest children's literature, by authors such as Mark Twain, Eleanor Clymer, and Langston Hughes.

Instead of excerpts, students in *Reading Mastery* read complete stories and poems, and even six novels, including such classics as *Tom Sawyer,* and *The Wizard of Oz.* The program also encourages outside reading by providing challenging study materials for award-winning modern novels, such as *Charlotte's Web* and *Island of the Blue Dolphins.*

Students in *Reading Mastery* are also writing, writing, writing. From the very beginning of the program, students write their own complete answers to questions, instead of circling somebody else's. By the upper levels, students are not only answering questions but also writing at least one paragraph a day on issues related to their reading. They are asked to reflect, to compare, to evaluate, to think. Bit by bit, they become full participants in the vibrant processes of writing, and reading.

Masters of the Reading Arts!

From the introduction of the letter **a** in the very first lesson . . . to Huckleberry Finn's concluding speech in the very last, *Reading Mastery* provides a consistent and commanding instructional plan. Throughout the program, the readings increase in length and complexity, the questions become more probing, the skill exercises more demanding, and the writing assignments more challenging. The daily lessons provide a thorough integration of all activities, and the materials that students bring home show daily progress.

Progress. In *Reading Mastery,* it happens each and every day. It begins with a single letter and it ends with students who can truly be called Masters of the Reading Arts.

The Programs

Materials

For the teacher:

- *Presentation Books* (all levels)

  These books contain presentation scripts for every lesson. The scripts tell the teacher what to say and do. The scripts also specify the students' answers. Many scripts provide specific procedures for correcting the students' mistakes. In levels II through VI, the *Presentation Books* also contain reproductions of the student material.

- *Teacher's Guides* (all levels)

  These guides explain the programs in detail and suggest specific teaching techniques for many of the program activities. The guides also contain correction procedures, suggestions for classroom management, and other material helpful to the teacher.

- *Behavioral Objectives* (all levels)

  A complete listing of the behavioral objectives for each skill taught in the program.

- *Skills Profile Folders* (all levels)

  Individual folders that allow the teacher to keep track of each student's skill mastery.

- *Teacher's Take-Home Books* (levels I–II)

  These books contain answer keys for the student *Take-Home Books.* [work]

- *Spelling Books* (levels I–II)

  These books contain optional spelling lessons that can be presented after the other program activities are completed. 10-12 minutes review from lesson

- *Testing and Management Handbooks* (optional–all levels)

  These handbooks are used with the optional *Test Books.* They contain instructions for administering the tests, a series of remedial exercises, and a Group Point Chart.

For the students:

- *Storybooks* (levels I–II)

- *Textbooks* (levels III–VI)

  These nonconsumable books contain the stories, novels, poems, biographies, comprehension passages, and factual articles that the students read.

- *Take-Home Books* (levels I–II)

  These consumable books contain questions and exercises that the students complete during each lesson. The students write the answers to *Take-Home Book* questions in the *Take-Home Book.* There is one perforated page for each lesson. After the students complete a page, the teacher checks their work. Then the students take the page home to show to their parents or guardians.

- *Workbooks* (levels III–VI)

  These consumable books contain questions about the *Textbook* stories, as well as vocabulary and skill exercises. Students write the answers to *Workbook* questions in the *Workbook.*

- *Skillbooks* (levels IV–VI)

  These nonconsumable books contain word lists, story questions, skill exercises, and independent activities. Students write the answers to *Skillbook* questions on a separate piece of paper.

- *Test Books* (optional–all levels)

  These consumable books contain a series of mastery tests that measure student progress throughout each program. They also contain an Individual Skills Profile Chart that the students use to keep track of their progress.

Activities

Every lesson in *Reading Mastery* consists of teacher-directed activities and independent student activities.

Teacher-Directed Activities

- **Prereading Exercises** (levels I–II)

  The students learn letter sounds and master decoding and comprehension readiness skills.

- **Word Practice** (all levels)

  The students read lists of words aloud, both in unison and individually. These words will later appear in the reading selections.

- **Vocabulary Exercises** (levels III–VI)

  The students learn the meanings of difficult words that will later appear in the reading selections.

- **Skill Exercises** (all levels)

  The teacher explains the skill exercises contained in the students' *Take-Homes, Workbooks,* or *Skillbooks.*

- **Group Reading** (all levels)

  The students take turns reading aloud from their *Storybooks* or *Textbooks.*

- **Comprehension Questions** (all levels)

  Both during and after the group reading, the teacher presents comprehension questions about the reading.

- **Individual Reading Checkouts** (levels I–V)

  In selected lessons, the teacher measures each student's decoding rate and accuracy.

- **Workcheck** (all levels)

  The teacher checks the students' independent work.

- **Spelling** (levels I–II)

  The teacher conducts optional spelling activities.

Independent Student Activities

- **Silent Reading** (all levels)

  The students read stories, questions, and exercises silently.

- **Story Items** (all levels)

  The students answer questions about the stories.

- **Skill Items** (all levels)

  The students complete exercises that teach specific decoding, comprehension, literary, and study skills.

- **Vocabulary Items** (levels III–VI)

  The students use new vocabulary words to complete sentences and work crossword puzzles.

- **Review Items** (all levels)

  The students review previously taught skills and vocabulary.

- **Fact Games** (levels III–V)

  The students play games that involve facts they have learned.

- **Special Projects** (levels IV–VI)

  The students complete special projects that relate to their reading selections.

- **Writing Assignments** (levels IV–VI)

  The students write paragraphs on assigned topics.

- **Supplementary Novels** (levels III–VI)

  The students read novels independently and complete comprehension activities for each novel.

Reading Mastery I

Reading Mastery I contains 160 daily lessons that teach basic decoding and comprehension skills. Decoding is taught through an explicit phonics method that stresses letter sounds and blending. Students practice decoding by reading word lists and stories, both aloud and silently. Comprehension activities include answering questions about pictures, following directions, and responding to a variety of questions based on the stories.

Materials

For the teacher:

- *Presentation Books* (3)
- *Teacher's Guide*
- *Spelling Book*
- *Teacher's Take-Home Book*
- *Behavioral Objectives Booklet*
- *Skills Profile Folder*
- A cassette demonstrating how to pronounce the sounds and how to present tasks from the program.

For the students:

- *Storybooks* (3)
- *Take-Home Books* (3)

The *Storybooks* contain original stories written especially for the program. There are both realistic and fantasy stories about animals and people.

Sample Activities   (first half)

In the first half of *Reading Mastery I* the students master decoding and comprehension readiness skills, learn individual letter sounds, and learn how to read regularly spelled words.

The following tasks from lesson 34 are typical of those found in the first half of the program. Task 1 (shown below) prepares the students for decoding by teaching them how to pronounce specific sounds. First the teacher says a sound; then the students say the sound in unison. The teacher uses a simple signal to make sure the students respond together. After the group has mastered the sound, individual students say the sound.

Task 1 also prepares the students for comprehension by teaching them how to follow directions. Every task in the *Presentation Books* involves directions that the students must follow.

TASK 1   Children say the sounds

- **a.** You're going to say some sounds. When I hold up my finger, say (pause) **c**. Get ready. Hold up one finger. **c**.
- **b.** Next sound. Say (pause) *iii*. Get ready. Hold up one finger. *iii*.
- **c.** Next sound. Say (pause) *nnn*. Get ready. Hold up one finger. *nnn*.
- **d.** Repeat *c* for sounds **c**, *iii*, and *nnn*.
- **e.** Call on different children to do *a*, *b*, or *c*.
- **f.** Good saying the sounds.

Task 2 teaches the students how to read the letter **i**. The teacher holds the *Presentation Book* so that the students can see the large **i**. First the teacher touches under the **i** and says the letter's sound: **iii**. Then the students say the sound in unison as the teacher touches under the letter. The students practice saying the sound until every student has mastered it. Finally, individual students say the sound.

A new letter sound is introduced every few lessons. The students learn every lower-case letter, as well as the sound combinations **th, sh, ch, ing, er, oo, wh**, and **qu**, and the word **I**. Long and short vowels are treated as separate letters. For example, short *a* (as in *mat*) is taught in lesson 1, and it always looks like this: **a**. Long *a* (as in *mate*) is taught in lesson 58, and it always has a macron over it: **ā**. In *Reading Mastery II*, the students learn other ways of distinguishing between long and short vowels, and the macron is no longer used.

TASK 2   Introducing the new sound i as in if

a. Touch the first ball of the arrow for **i**. Here's a new sound. My turn to say it. Get ready. Move quickly to the second ball. Hold. **iii**.

b. Return to the first ball. My turn again. Get ready. Move quickly to the second ball. Hold. **iii**.

c. Return to the first ball. My turn again. Get ready. Move quickly to the second ball. Hold. **iii**.

d. Return to the first ball. Your turn. Get ready. Move quickly to the second ball. Hold. *iii*. Yes, **iii**.

e. Return to the first ball. Again. Get ready. Move quickly to the second ball. Hold. *iii*. Yes, **iii**.

f. Repeat *e* until firm.

g. Call on different children to do *d*.

h. Good saying **iii**.

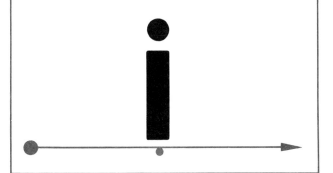

In task 13, the students learn how to read a regularly spelled word. First the students identify the individual letter sounds in the word. Then they sound out the word. Finally, they read the word by "saying it fast."

This simple and effective sounding-out procedure allows the students to read hundreds of regularly spelled words.

TASK 13   Children say the sounds, then sound out the word

a. Touch the first ball of the arrow for **am**. You're going to sound it out. Point to the ball for **a**. What sound are you going to say first? Touch the ball. *aaa*. Yes, **aaa**. Point to the ball for **m**. What sound are you going to say next? Touch the ball. *mmm*. Yes, **mmm**.

b. Return to the first ball. Everybody, when I move my finger, say the sounds **aaammm**. Don't stop between the sounds. Get ready. Move quickly under each sound. Hold. *Aaammm*.

c. Return to the first ball. Again. Sound it out. Get ready. Move quickly under each sound. Hold. *Aaammm*.

d. Repeat *c* until firm.

e. Return to the first ball. Say it fast. Slash. *Am.*
Yes, **am**. You read the word **am**. Do you know who I (pause) **am**?

f. Call on different children to do *c* and *e*.

After they finish the *Presentation Book* activities, the students complete exercises in their *Take-Home Books*. The *Take-Home Book* exercises develop and expand the skills taught in the *Presentation Book*. First the teacher goes over the exercises with the students; then the students complete the exercises on their own. In the tasks shown below, the students follow pictured directions, copy letters, pair letters with objects, and complete a picture.

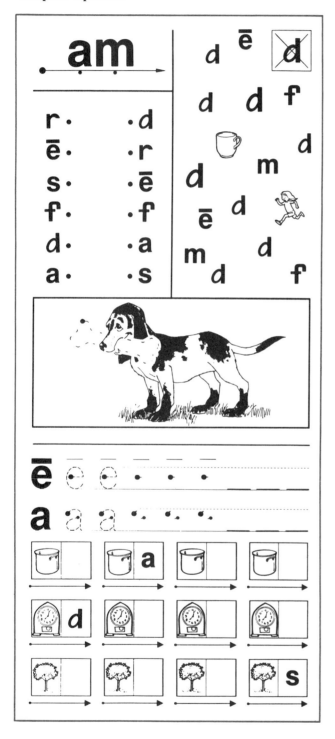

Sample Activities (second half)

In the second half of *Reading Mastery I*, the students read complete stories, answer comprehension questions, and learn how to read a number of irregular words.

The following tasks from lessons 113 and 115 are typical of those found in the second half of the program.

By the second half of the program, the students have learned almost all the lower-case letters, as well as several sound combinations. In the task shown below, the teacher presents the sound combination **ch**. The two letters that make up this sound are connected by a heavy black line. This unique orthography is used for all sound combinations in *Reading Mastery I*. In *Reading Mastery II*, the students learn other means of recognizing sound combinations, and the letters are disjoined.

ch

TASK 1 Teaching ch as in chat

a. Point to **ch**. Here's a new sound. It's a quick sound.
b. My turn. (Pause.) Touch **ch** for an instant, saying: ch. Do not say chuh.
c. Again. Touch **ch** and say: ch.
d. Point to **ch**. Your turn. When I touch it, you say it. (Pause.) **Get ready.** Touch **ch**. *ch*.
e. Again. Touch **ch**. *ch*.
f. Repeat *e* until firm.

The students continue to learn new regularly spelled words. They also learn how to read irregular words, how to read words "the fast way," and how to read words in lists. The *Presentation Book* page below contains a typical group of tasks.

In task 11, the students read an irregular word: **arm**. First the students sound out the word. Then the teacher tells the students how to say the word correctly. Finally, the students practice reading the word.

A new irregular word is introduced every few lessons. The program teaches more than fifty irregular words.

In tasks 12 and 13, the students read a word that rhymes with *arm*: **farm**. Because this new word is so similar to the word presented before, the students are able to read the new word without first sounding it out.

In task 14, students sound out and read the word **teach**. The *a* is smaller than the other letters in the word. The students have already learned that, "When a word has a little sound, you don't say the sound." This rule allows the students to sound out words with silent letters. In *Reading Mastery II*, the students learn other means of identifying silent letters, and all letters become the same size.

In task 15, the students read all the words on the page "the fast way." When they read words "the fast way," the students simply read the words without sounding them out. Finally, in task 16, individual students take turns reading the words.

TASK 11 Children sound out an irregular word (arm)

a. Touch the ball for **arm**. Sound it out.
b. Get ready. Quickly touch each sound as the children say *aaarrrmmm*.
c. Again. Repeat *b* until firm.
d. That's how we <u>sound out</u> the word. Here's how we <u>say</u> the word.
  Arm. How do we <u>say</u> the word? (Signal.) *Arm*.
e. Now you're going to <u>sound out</u> the word. Get ready.
  Touch each sound as the children say *aaarrrmmm*.
f. Now you're going to <u>say</u> the word. Get ready. (Signal.) *Arm*.
g. Repeat *e* and *f* until firm.

TASK 12 Children rhyme with an irregular word (arm)

a. Touch the ball for **arm**. Everybody, you're going to read this
  word the fast way. Get ready. (Signal.) *Arm*.
b. Touch the ball for **farm**. This word rhymes with (pause) **arm**.
  Get ready. Move to **f**, then quickly along the arrow. *Farm*.
c. Repeat *a* and *b* until firm.

TASK 13 Children sound out farm

Have the children sound out **farm**. *Fffaaarrrmmm*. How do we say the
  word? (Signal.) *Farm*. Yes, **farm**. Do you live on a **farm**?

TASK 14 Children sound out the word and tell what word

a. Touch the ball for **tēach**. Sound it out.
b. Get ready. Touch **t, ē, ch** as the children say *tēēēch*.
  If sounding out is not firm, repeat *b*.
c. What word? (Signal.) *Teach*. Yes, **teach**.

TASK 15 Children read the words the fast way

a. Now you get to read the words on this page the fast way.
b. Touch the ball for **arm**. (Pause three seconds.) Get ready.
  Move your finger quickly along the arrow. *Arm*.
c. Repeat *b* for each word on the page.

TASK 16 Individual test

Call on different children to read one word the fast way.

Do not touch any small letters.

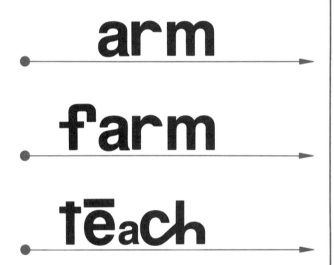

Beginning in lesson 91, the students read entire stories in their *Storybooks*. These stories are written with words that the students have already learned. Initially, the stories are only a few sentences long. By the end of the program, however, the students are reading longer stories that are serialized over a span of lessons.

The story-reading activities for lesson 115 are shown below. In task 21, the teacher reads the title of the story. The students learn that the title tells what the story is going to be about. In task 22, the students read the entire story "the fast way," without sounding out any words. After they finish this first reading, the students review any words they had trouble with. Then, in task 24, they read the story again, as the teacher asks literal and interpretive comprehension questions.

Most of the teacher's questions can be answered by specific words in the story. The students answer these questions in unison, at the teacher's signal. Some questions, however, require the students to make personal judgements or predictions. These questions are answered by individual students.

After the students finish the story, they predict what a picture of the story would look like. Then they turn the page and look at a picture of the story. The teacher presents comprehension questions about the picture. Later, the students will draw their own picture of the story.

On the *Take-Home* for lesson 115 (shown on the next page), the students copy letters and sentences, match words, follow pictured directions, and associate words with pictures. They also draw a picture of the day's story in the blank space on side 2. The teacher explains all of the exercises before the students complete them.

Lesson 115 also includes an individual reading checkout (shown on the next page). The checkout requires the students to read for rate and accuracy. As the group is working independently, the teacher calls on individual students to read the day's story aloud. The students earn stars if they can read the entire story in less than two minutes, while making no more than three errors.

---

lots of cars

a man on a farm has lots of

cars. hē has ōld cars. hē has

littlе cars.

arе his cars fōr gōаts? nō.

arе his cars fōr shēēp? nō. arе

his cars fōr cows? nō.

his cars arе fōr cops. hē has

lots of cop cars.

TASK 21   Teacher introduces the title

a. Pass out Storybook 1.
b. Open your book to page 56.
c. Hold up your reader. Point to the title. These words are called the title of the story. These words tell what the story is about. I'll read the title the fast way.
d. Point to the words as you read: Lots of cars.
e. Everybody, what is this story about? (Signal.) *Lots of cars.*
   Yes, **lots of cars**. This story is going to tell something about **lots of cars**.

TASK 22   First reading—children read the story the fast way

Have the children reread any sentences containing words that give them trouble. Keep a list of these words.

a. Everybody, touch the title of the story and get ready to read the words in the title the fast way.
b. First word. Check children's responses. (Pause three seconds.) Get ready. Clap. *Lots.*
c. Next word. Check children's responses. (Pause three seconds.) Get ready. Clap. *Of.*
d. Repeat c for the word **cars**.
e. After the children have read the title, ask: What's this story about? (Signal.) *Lots of cars.* Yes, **lots of cars**.
f. Everybody, touch the first word of the story. Check children's responses.
g. Get ready to read this story the fast way.
h. First word. (Pause three seconds.) Get ready. Clap. *A.*
i. Next word. Check children's responses. (Pause three seconds.) Get ready. Clap. *Man.*
j. Repeat i for the remaining words in the first sentence. Pause at least three seconds between claps. The children are to identify each word without sounding it out.
k. Repeat h through j for the next two sentences. Have the children reread the first three sentences until firm.
l. The children are to read the remainder of the story the fast way, stopping at the end of each sentence.
m. After the first reading of the story, print on the board the words that the children missed more than one time. Have the children sound out each word one time and tell what word.
n. After the group's responses are firm, call on individual children to read the words.

TASK 23 Individual test

a. Look at page 56. I'm going to call on different children to read
a whole sentence the fast way.
b. Call on different children to read a sentence. Do not clap for
each word.

TASK 24 Second reading—children read the story the fast way and answer questions

a. You're going to read the story again the fast way and I'll ask
questions.
b. Starting with the first word of the title. *Check children's responses.
Get ready. Clap. Lots.*
c. Clap for each remaining word. Pause at least three seconds between
claps. Pause longer before words that gave the children trouble
during the first reading.
d. Ask the comprehension questions below as the children read.

After the children read:	You say:
Lots of cars.	What's this story about? (Signal.) *Lots of cars.*
A man on a farm has lots of cars.	What does he have? (Signal.) *Lots of cars.*
He has little cars.	What kind of cars does he have? (Signal.) *Old cars and little cars.*
Are his cars for goats?	What do you think? *The children respond.* Let's read and find out.
No.	Are they for goats? (Signal.) *No.*
He has lots of cop cars.	What kind of cars does he have? (Signal.) *Cop cars.*

TASK 25 Picture comprehension

a. What do you think you'll see in the picture? *The children respond.*
b. Turn the page and look at the picture.
c. Ask these questions:
   1. Do you see lots of cop cars? *Yes.*
   2. What would you do if you had all those cop cars?
   The children respond.

TASK 33 2-minute individual checkout

a. As you are doing your take-home, I'll call on children one at a time
to read the **whole story.** Remember, you get two stars if you read
the story in less than two minutes and make no more than three
errors.
b. Call on a child. Tell the child: Start with the title and read the story
carefully the fast way. Go. Time the child. Tell the child any words
the child misses. Stop the child as soon as the child makes the fourth
error or exceeds the time limit.
c. If the child meets the rate-accuracy criterion, record two stars on
your chart for lesson 115. Congratulate the child. Give children who
do not earn two stars a chance to read the story again before the
next lesson is presented.

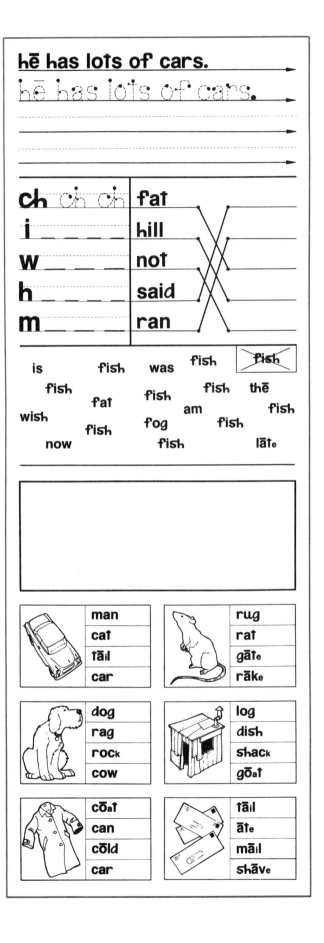

Reading Mastery II

Reading Mastery II contains 160 daily lessons that expand basic reading skills. Students in the program learn strategies for decoding difficult words and for answering interpretive comprehension questions. They also learn basic reasoning skills, such as making inferences and drawing conclusions. The daily reading selections include realistic fiction, fantasy, and factual articles.

Materials

For the teacher:

- *Presentation Books* (3)
- *Teacher's Guide*
- *Teacher's Take-Home Book*
- *Spelling Book*
- *Behavioral Objectives Booklet*
- *Skills Profile Folder*

For the students:

- *Storybooks* (2)
- *Take-Home Books* (3)

The *Storybooks* contain original stories written especially for the program, as well as adaptations of famous children's stories. Many of the stories are serialized over a span of lessons.

Sample Activities

Each lesson in *Reading Mastery II* begins with word practice tasks. These tasks appear in the *Presentation Book*. In the first part of the program, the teacher presents individual sounds and words, and the students read them aloud. Later in the program, the teacher presents lists of words that the students read aloud.

In lessons 1-47, the unique *Reading Mastery I* orthography is used for all words. In lessons 48-92, the *Reading Mastery I* orthography is gradually phased out and replaced by standard orthography. During this transition period, the students learn the final-e rule and other guides for reading words in standard orthography. They also learn every capital letter. In lessons 93-160, standard orthography is used in all the student materials.

The following activities appear in lesson 97. The lesson begins with four separate word lists. The list in task 1 contains new words that are difficult to decode, as well as words that the students have already learned. The new words are printed in red. The teacher first reads the new words; then the students spell them. Finally, the students read the new words. After the students have mastered the new words, they read the entire list.

The students read all of the words in unison. When the teacher points to a word, the students look over the word and get ready to read it. Then they read the word in unison as the teacher slashes under the word with a finger.

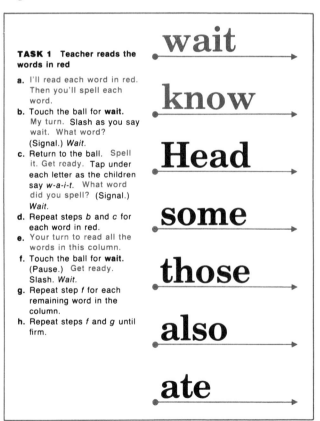

In task 2, the students read words that contain various sound combinations, word endings, or root words. These word elements are underlined in each word. The students first read the underlined part; then they read the entire word.

These underlined-part word lists teach students an important decoding strategy. The lists demonstrate that many unfamiliar words are made up of familiar parts. By identifying these familiar parts, the students are able to decode unfamiliar words.

In task 3, the students read new words that are easy to decode or words that they have already learned. The teacher points to each word; then the students read the word when the teacher slashes under it with a finger.

In task 4, the students spell each word before reading it. This procedure not only promotes accurate spelling, but also teaches the students to examine words carefully.

After the group finishes reading all the lists, individual students take turns reading one list each.

TASK 2 Words with underlined parts

a. First you're going to read the underlined part of each word in this column. Then you're going to read the whole word.
b. Touch the ball for **string**. Read the underlined part. Get ready. Tap the ball. *Ing.* Read the whole word. (Pause.) Get ready. Slash. *String.*
c. Repeat step b until firm.
d. Repeat steps b and c for each remaining word in the column.
e. Repeat the column until children read all the words in order without making a mistake.

string

stand

stones

cash

TASK 3 Read the fast way

a. You're going to read all the words in this column the fast way.
b. Touch the ball for **Let's**. (Pause.) Get ready. Slash. *Let's.*
c. Repeat step b until firm.
d. Repeat steps b and c for each remaining word in the column.
e. Repeat the column until the children read all the words in order without making mistakes.

Let's

who

ice cream

didn't

hopping

But

Liked

TASK 4 Children spell, then read

a. First you're going to spell each word. Then you're going to read that word the fast way.
b. Touch the ball for **hoping**. Spell it. Get ready. Tap under each letter as the children say h-o-p-i-n-g. Return to the ball. Read it. Get ready. Slash. *Hoping.*
c. Repeat step b for each remaining word in the column.
d. Repeat steps b and c until firm.

hoping

tame

bite

then

cone

right

tiger

Individual test

a. Call on different children to read one column of words from the lesson.
b. Praise children who read all words with no errors.

After the word-practice tasks are completed, the teacher directs the students as they read aloud from their *Storybooks*. During this group reading, the teacher monitors the students' decoding accuracy and also presents comprehension questions.

The students begin the group reading by reading the first part of the story within a specified decoding error limit. The first part of the story extends from the title to the circled 5. The teacher calls on individual students to read two or three sentences in turn. The students must practice reading the story until they can read up to the circled 5 while making no more than five decoding errors.

The *Presentation Book* contains reproductions of the *Storybook* pages. Numbers are placed within these reproductions to indicate where the teacher is to present comprehension questions. The actual questions are printed under the reproduced pages.

After the group reads the first part of the story within the error limit, the teacher rereads the first part and presents the comprehension questions. Then the students take turns reading the rest of the story, as the teacher presents more comprehension questions.

The comprehension questions teach a variety of literal and interpretive comprehension skills. In this sample lesson, the students relate titles to story content, answer literal questions, identify the meanings of common words, and predict narrative outcomes.

TASK 5 Reading—decoding

a. Pass out Storybook 2.

b. Everybody, open your reader to page 38.

c. Remember, if the group reads all the way to the red 5 without making more than five errors, we can go on.

d. Everybody, touch the title of the story. Check.

e. If you hear a mistake, raise your hand. Remember, children who do not have their place lose their turn. Call on individual children to read two or three sentences. Do not ask comprehension questions. Tally all errors.

To correct word-identification errors (**from**, for example)

1. That word is **from**. What word? *From.*
2. Go back to the beginning of the sentence and read the sentence again.

f. If the children make more than five errors before they reach the red 5: when they reach the 5 return to the beginning of the story and have the children reread to the 5. Do not ask comprehension questions. Repeat step *f* until firm, and then go on to step *g.*

g. When the children read to the red 5 without making more than five errors: read the story to the children from the beginning to the 5. Ask the specified comprehension questions. When you reach the 5, call on individual children to continue reading the story. Have each child read two or three sentences. Ask the specified comprehension questions.

The Tame Tiger Who Liked Ice Cream[1]

There once was a tame tiger. This tiger did not bite children.[2] He didn't eat goats or sheep.[3] He said, "I like ice cream.[4] So I will go to town and get some."

But the tiger didn't have any cash.[5] He said, "I will fill my pouch with round stones. I hope that the man at the ice cream store likes round stones."[6]

So the tiger filled his pouch with round stones. Then he walked to town. He went up to the man at the ice cream stand.

"I don't have any cash," the tiger said. "But I have a pouch filled with pretty round stones."[7]

"Let's see them," the man said.

So the tiger showed the man his stones. The man said, "I like those stones. They are pretty."[8]

The tiger gave the pouch to the man.⑤

Then the tiger said, "I want a big cone, and I want some string."[9]

The man said, "What will you do with a big cone and some string?"

"Wait and see," the tiger said.

What do you think the tiger did?[10]He ate the ice cream from the cone.[11]Then he put the big cone on his head with a string.[12]

The tiger said, "I love ice cream and I love hats. I ate the ice cream and now I have the best hat in town."[13]

The man at the ice cream stand said, "That tiger is very tame. He is also very smart."

The end

[1]What is this story going to be about? (Signal.) *The tame tiger who liked ice cream.* A tiger is an animal with stripes.
[2]Did this tiger bite children? (Signal.) *No.* Right. He was tame.
[3]I wonder what he did eat? Let's read some more.
[4]Now we know. What does he eat? (Signal.) *Ice cream.*
[5]What didn't he have? (Signal.) *Cash.* What's cash? *The children respond.* Right. He didn't have any money.
[6]What does the tiger want to do with the round stones? *The children respond.*
[7]Does he have cash? (Signal.) *No.* What does he have? (Signal.) *Pretty round stones.*
[8]Did the man like those stones? (Signal.) *Yes.*
[9]What did the tiger say? (Signal.) *I want a big cone, and I want some string.*
[10]What do you think? *The children respond.* Let's keep reading.
[11]What's the first thing the tiger did? (Signal.) *He ate the ice cream.*
[12]What's the next thing he did? (Signal.) *The children respond.*
[13]How did he get that hat? *The children respond.* Right. He made it from the cone and string.

After the students finish reading the story, they complete written exercises in their *Take-Home Books*. In this sample lesson, the students answer questions about the story, follow written directions, and complete deductions. They also read a short passage and answer questions about the passage.

The teacher explains new exercises to the students. In this sample lesson, the teacher explains the deductions exercise. The students do the remaining exercises on their own.

TASK 7 Picture deductions

a. Pass out Take-Home 97 to each child.

b. Hold up side 2 of your take-home and touch the sentence in the box in the deductions exercise.

c. Everybody, touch this sentence on your take-home. Check children's responses.

d. Call on a child. Read the sentence in the box. *All the big horses are tired.*

e. Everybody, say that rule. (Signal.) *All the big horses are tired.* Repeat until firm.

f. You know that some of the horses in the picture are tired. What kind of horses are those? (Signal.) *All the big horses.* Everybody, touch a horse you know is tired. Check.

g. You don't know about the horses that are not big. Everybody, touch a horse you don't know about. Check.

h. Call on a child. Read the instructions below the box. *Circle every horse that is tired.*

i. Everybody, what are you going to do? (Signal.) *Circle every horse that is tired.* Yes, circle every horse that you know is tired.

j. Do it. Check.

TASK 8 Summary of independent activities

Everybody, now you'll do your take-home. Remember to do all parts of the take-home and to read all the parts carefully.

---

1. The tiger was _____ .
   lame   old   tame   time

2. Did he bite children? _____

3. What did he like to eat? _____
   ice   ice bits   ice cream   ice skates

4. Did the tiger have any cash? _____

5. What was in his pouch? _____
   stops   cones   stones   rocks

6. Did the man like the stones? _____

7. Who said, "What will you do with a big cone and some string"? _____

8. Who said, "Wait and see"? _____

9. The tiger made the cone into a h_____ .

> The boy felt cold in the rain.

1. Make a box around the word that tells how the boy felt.

2. Make a box around the words that tell where the boy is.

3. Make a line over the words that tell who felt cold.

One day, the boss left a note for Sid. Here is what that note said: "Tape my cane with a bit of white tape. The white tape is in the tape can."
Do you think Sid did what the note said? Yes, he did. After he looked at the note, he got the white tape and taped the cane.

1. Who left the note for Sid? _____

2. The note told Sid to _____ a cane.

3. Where was the white tape? _____
   in the tap can   in the tape can

4. Sid got the tape and taped the _____ .

> All the big horses are tired.

Circle every horse that is tired.

Reading Mastery III

Reading Mastery III contains 140 daily lessons that emphasize reasoning and reference skills. Students in the program learn how to apply rules in a wide variety of contexts and how to interpret maps, graphs, and time lines. The program also introduces a number of complex sentence forms and a range of vocabulary activities. The daily reading selections include realistic fiction, fantasy, and factual articles.

Materials

For the teacher:

- *Presentation Books* (2)
- *Teacher's Guide*

For the students:

- *Textbooks* (2)
- *Workbooks* (2)

The *Textbooks* contain stories and comprehension passages written especially for the program. Most of the stories are serialized over a span of lessons, and many of the stories incorporate science facts and rules. Here is a partial listing of the *Textbook* contents.

- **A Tricky Toad Named Goad** - A toad has amusing adventures in which she tricks people.
- **Nancy Learns About Being Small** - A girl becomes very small and learns important facts about common objects.
- **Herman Travels the World** - A fly goes around the world on a jet. The students use maps to follow the jet's progress.
- **Linda and Kathy Alone on an Island** - Two girls are shipwrecked and struggle to survive on an island.
- **Bertha and Her Nose** – A girl with a great sense of smell helps an investigator capture a group of polluters.
- **Andrew Dexter's Dreams** - A bank teller gets superhuman powers and is hired by a football team.
- **The Time Machine** - Two boys find a time machine and go back and forth in time.
- **Comprehension Passages** - Short passages that provide background information for the stories.

Sample Activities

The following activities appear in lesson 24 of *Reading Mastery III*.

The students begin lesson 24 — and every lesson — by reading word lists. There are four types of lists. The first type consists of words that are difficult to decode. The teacher reads these words to the students. Then the students read the words and spell them.

The second type of list consists of words that have a common feature, such as a common sound or a common ending. The teacher explains the common feature; then the students read the words.

The third type of list consists of words that are easy to decode or words that the students have already learned. The teacher simply directs the students to read these lists.

The last type of list consists of vocabulary words that will later appear in the reading selections. The students first read these words; then the teacher explains what the words mean. The students then practice using the words in sentences.

A

1	2	3	4
wild	action	boasted	already
silence	mansion	removed	Toadsville
group	impression	escaped	hundreds
women	motion	Alaska	shovel
swallow	mention	escaping	fourth
tongue			

5	6	7	8
half	balloon	warts	**Vocabulary**
second	ground	covered	**words**
breath	underground	rough	1. escape
third	crazy	stubby	2. favorite
taste		clearly	

EXERCISE 1   Word practice

1. Everybody, find part A in your textbook. *Wait.* Touch column 1. *Check.* The words in column 1 are hard words that will be in your reading stories.
2. Touch under the first word. *Check.* The first word is **wild.**
   What word? *Signal.* **Wild.**
   Spell **wild.** *Signal.* **W-i-l-d.**
   What word did you spell? *Signal.* **Wild.**
3. Next word. *Pause.* That word is **silence.**
   What word? *Signal.* **Silence.**
   Spell **silence.** *Signal.* **S-i-l-e-n-c-e.**
   What word did you spell? *Signal.* **Silence.**
4. *Repeat step 3 for each remaining word in column 1.*
5. Now let's see if you remember all those words. Touch under the first word in column 1. *Pause.* What word? *Signal.* **Wild.**
6. Next word. *Pause.*
   What word? *Signal.* **Silence.**
7. *Repeat step 6 for each remaining word in column 1.*
8. *Repeat the words in column 1 until firm.*

EXERCISE 2   Sound combinations

1. Everybody, touch column 2. *Check.* All the words in column 2 end with the sound **shun.**
   What sound? *Signal.* **Shun.** The first word is **action.**
   What word? *Signal.* **Action.**
   Spell **action.** *Signal.* **A-c-t-i-o-n.**
   What word did you spell? *Signal.* **Action.**
   The letters **t-i-o-n** make the sound **shun** in that word.
2. The next word is **mansion.**
   What word? *Signal.* **Mansion.**
   Spell **mansion.** *Signal.* **M-a-n-s-i-o-n.**
   What word did you spell? *Signal.* **Mansion.**
   The letters **s-i-o-n** make the sound **shun** in that word.
3. The next word is **impression.**
   What word? *Signal.* **Impression.**
   Spell **impression.** *Signal.* **I-m-p-r-e-s-s-i-o-n.**
   What word did you spell? *Signal.* **Impression.**
   What letters make the sound **shun** in **impression?** *Signal.* **S-i-o-n.**
4. *Repeat step 3 for each remaining word in column 2.*
5. Now let's see if you remember all those words. Touch under the first word. *Pause.*
   What word? *Signal.* **Action.**
6. Next word. *Pause.* What word? *Signal.* **Mansion.**
7. *Repeat step 6 for each remaining word in column 2.*
8. *Repeat the words in column 2 until firm.*

EXERCISE 3   Word practice

1. Everybody, touch under the first word in column 3. Spell the word. Get ready. *Signal.* **B-o-a-s-t-e-d.**
   What sound do the letters **o-a** make in that word? *Signal.* **Ō.**
   Read the word. Get ready. *Signal.* **Boasted.**
2. Next word. *Pause.* What word? *Signal.* **Removed.**
3. *Repeat step 2 for each remaining word in column 3.*
4. *Repeat the words in column 3 until firm.*
5. Touch under the first word in column 4. *Pause.* What word? *Signal.* **Already.**
6. Next word. *Pause.* What word? *Signal.* **Toadsville.**
7. *Repeat step 6 for each remaining word in column 4.*
8. *Repeat the words in column 4 until firm.*
9. *Repeat steps 5–8 for columns 5–7.*

EXERCISE 4   Vocabulary words

Task A
1. Everybody, touch column 8. *Check.* First you're going to read the words in column 8. Then we'll talk about what they mean.
2. Touch under the first word. *Pause.* What word? *Signal.* **Escape.**
3. Next word. *Pause.* What word? *Signal.* **Favorite.**

Task B
1. Now let's talk about what those words mean. Word 1 is **escape.** When you **escape** from something, you get away from it. Here's another way of saying **She got away from the robber: She escaped from the robber.**
2. Your turn. What's another way of saying **She got away from the robber?** *Signal.*
   She escaped from the robber.
   Repeat step 2 until firm.
3. What's another way of saying **Goad got away from the trap?** *Signal.*
   Goad escaped from the trap.

Task C
1. Word 2 is **favorite.** If something is your **favorite** thing, it's the thing you like best. Another way of saying **the cake she likes best** is **her favorite cake.**
2. Your turn. What's another way of saying **the cake she likes best?** *Signal.* **Her favorite cake.**
   Repeat step 2 until firm.
3. What's another way of saying **the game he likes best?** *Signal.* **His favorite game.** What's another way of saying **the story they like best?** *Signal.* **Their favorite story.**

After the students complete the word-list activities, they read their *Textbook* stories aloud. Many of these stories are preceded by comprehension passages. The comprehension passages present background information for the stories. The students will make use of this information as they read the stories.

The students read the comprehension passage aloud. Individual students take turns reading two or three sentences each. Some sentences in the passage are followed by a circled letter. When a student reads to a circled letter, the teacher presents comprehension questions for that letter from the *Presentation Book*. These questions teach a variety of comprehension, reference, and study skills.

After they finish the comprehension passage, the students read the story aloud within specified decoding error limits. These error limits are indicated by signs that appear in the text.

There are two kinds of error signs. The first is the 2-error sign. This sign always appears after the first part of the story, and it indicates that the students must read the first part of the story while making no more than two decoding errors. If the students go over the 2-error limit, they reread the first part until they can stay within the limit.

The second kind of error sign is the story-error sign. This sign always appears at the end of the story. The error number varies with the length of the story. If the students can read the entire story within the story-error limit, they earn points.

As the students read the story, the teacher presents comprehension questions from the *Presentation Book*. These questions are cued by the circled letters in the student text.

The comprehension questions in *Reading Mastery III* emphasize interpretive comprehension skills, reasoning skills, and study skills. In this sample lesson, the students interpret titles, infer story details, infer causes and effects, and predict outcomes.

After the students finish the *Textbook* activities, they work independently in the *Workbook*. The independent work includes items about the comprehension passage, story items, skill items, and review items.

The comprehension-passage items and story items are based on the comprehension questions presented during the group reading. In this sample lesson, the students recall narrative details, classify objects, explain causes and effects, and infer narrative events. Story items in other lessons involve skills such as sequencing narrative events, inferring details, and interpreting motives.

The skill items teach reasoning skills. In this sample lesson, the students make comparisons and complete deductions.

The review items review previously taught facts and skills. In this sample lesson, the students review map-reading skills.

B

More Facts about Toads and Frogs

Toads and frogs are members of the same family. But toads are different from frogs. Here are some facts about how they are different:

- Toads have skin that is rough and covered with warts. Ⓐ
- Toads have no teeth. Ⓑ
- The back legs of toads are not as big or strong. Ⓒ

C

Goad Uses Her First Trick Ⓐ

*Goad lived near Four Mile Lake. Down the road from the lake was a town. The name of that town was Toadsville. It was named Toadsville because so many people who visited the town had come to hunt for a big, smart, fast toad. Ⓑ And in the evening you could find hundreds of people sitting around Toadsville talking about Goad. First they would talk about some of the traps that had been made to catch Goad. Then they would tell how Goad escaped. One of their favorite stories is the one of the great big net. Ⓒ ✿ 2 ERRORS ✿

Five hunters from Alaska* had come to Four Mile Lake with a net that was nearly a mile wide. They waited until Goad was on a hill where there were no trees, just some white rocks. Then they flew over the hill in a plane and dropped the great big net over the hill. Ⓓ Goad was under the net. The five hunters rushed to the place where Goad had last been seen. But there was no Goad. There was some grass and five large white rocks. The hunters removed the net and began to go over every centimeter of the ground. Ⓔ Suddenly, one of the hunters noticed that the biggest rock was moving. The biggest rock wasn't a rock at all. It was Goad.

She had moved near the other rocks. Then she had turned over on her back so that her white belly was showing. That belly looked like a white rock. Suddenly she turned over. "There she is," one of the hunters yelled, but before the others could turn around, Goad hopped down the side of the hill and was gone. Ⓕ ✿ 6 ERRORS ✿

EXERCISE 6 Reading: comprehension

1. Everybody, find part B in your textbook. *Wait.*
2. *Call on individual students to read two or three sentences, starting with the title. Present the tasks specified for the circled letters.*

Comprehension tasks

Ⓐ Everybody, what is a toad's skin covered with? *Signal.* **Warts.**

● Warts are like rough bumps. Everybody, do frogs have skin that is rough and covered with warts? *Signal.* **No.**

Ⓑ Everybody, listen to that fact again. Toads have no teeth. Say that fact. *Signal. Repeat until firm.*

● Everybody, do frogs have teeth? *Signal.* **Yes.**

● Everybody, do toads have teeth? *Signal.* **No.**

Ⓒ Everybody, whose back legs are stronger, toads or frogs? *Signal.* **Frogs.**

EXERCISE 7 Reading: decoding

1. Everybody, find part C in your textbook. *Wait. Call on a student.*
   What's the error limit for this story? **6 errors.**
2. *Call on individual students to read two or three sentences, starting with the title.*

Comprehension tasks

Ⓐ *Call on a student.* What's going to happen in this story? *Idea:* Goad will use her first trick.

Ⓑ Everybody, who is that big, smart, fast toad? *Signal.* **Goad.**

Ⓒ *Call on a student.* How could you use a great big net to catch a toad? *Idea:* Drop it on top of the toad, etc.

Ⓓ Do you think that Goad was fast enough to get away before the net landed? *Call on individual students. Responses:* Student preference.

Ⓔ The picture shows the hunters looking for Goad. You can see the trick that Goad is using. *Call on a student.* What is she doing? *Idea:* Pretending to be a rock.

Ⓕ *Call on a student.* Why didn't those hunters just grab her when she was hopping down the hill? *Idea:* Goad was too fast.

LESSON 24

ERRORS	WA	G	WB	BONUS	T

A

In today's lesson, you read about how toads are different from frogs. Use what you learned to do these items.

1. **a.** Which animal can jump farther, a toad or a frog? _____

   b. How do you know? _____

2. Which animal feels smooth, a toad or a frog? _____

3. Which animal has teeth, a toad or a frog? _____

4. **Circle** the toads in the picture.

B

Story items

5. **Fill in the blanks.**

   a. Goad was hard to catch because she was very _____

   b. She was also very _____

   c. She was also very _____

6. What did the hunters from Alaska use when they tried to catch Goad? _____

7. What trick did Goad use to fool the hunters from Alaska?

   _____

8. What part of Goad is white? _____

9. **Circle** the picture that could be Goad using her first trick.

Skill items

10. Look at object A, object B, and object C. Write two ways all three objects are the same. ① _____

    ② _____

    Object A   Object B   Object C

11. Here's a rule: **Tadpoles have a tail.**

    a. A cat is not a tadpole. So what else do you know about a cat? _____

    b. Sam is a tadpole. So what else do you know about Sam? _____

    c. Pam is not a tadpole. So what else do you know about Pam? _____

    d. Jean is a tadpole. So what else do you know about Jean? _____

Review items

12. **a.** Write **north, south, east,** and **west** in the right boxes.

    b. Touch the X. An arrow goes from the X. Which direction is that arrow going? _____

    c. Make an arrow that goes west from the Y.

    d. Make an arrow that goes south from the Z.

Reading Mastery IV

Reading Mastery IV contains 140 daily lessons that emphasize problem-solving skills and reading in the content areas. Students in the program evaluate problems and solutions, learn facts about the world, and complete research projects. Many of the daily reading selections incorporate facts from science and social studies.

Materials

For the teacher:

- *Presentation Books* (2)
- *Teacher's Guide*

For the students:

- *Textbook*
- *Skillbook*
- *Workbook*

The *Textbook* contains stories, factual articles, and comprehension passages written especially for the program. All of the stories are serialized over a span of lessons. Most of the stories incorporate science facts and rules. Here is a partial listing of the *Textbook* contents.

- **Toby the Kangaroo** - An imaginative story about kangaroos in Australia.
- **Oomoo, Oolak, and a Polar Bear** - A realistic story about Alaskan Eskimos.
- **Leonard the Inventor** - A realistic story about a boy who invents things.
- **A Trip Through the Solar System** - A science-fiction story.
- **Waldo the Animal Trainer** - A realistic story about a boy who trains animals.
- **Go Anywhere - See Anything** - An imaginative story about two children who can go anywhere and see anything.
- **Comprehension Passages** - Short passages that provide background information for the stories.
- **Factual Articles** - Articles about people and the world.

Sample Activities

The following activities appear in lesson 46 of *Reading Mastery IV.*

The students begin lesson 46 — and every lesson — by reading word lists. There are four types: lists of words that are difficult to decode; lists of words with common features; lists of words that are easy to decode; and lists of vocabulary words.

The teacher directs the students as they read these lists in unison. Then the teacher explains the vocabulary words, and the students practice using them in context. Finally, individual students take turns reading one list each.

A

1	2	3
energy	beam	hollered
device	reaching	crossed
arithmetic	wearing	giggled
solution	teacher	coughed
assignment	bear	

4	5	6
draw	sad	**Vocabulary words**
difficult	sadly	1. sour face
tone	stink	2. save energy
drawings	solve	3. enter
	stinks	4. solution

EXERCISE 1 Word practice

1. Everybody, find lesson 46, part A in your textbook. *Wait.* Touch column 1. *Check.* The words in column 1 are hard words that will be in your reading stories.
2. Touch under the first word. *Check.* The first word is **energy.** What word? *Signal.* **Energy.** Spell **energy.** *Signal.* **E-n-e-r-g-y.** What word did you spell? *Signal.* **Energy.**
3. Next word. *Pause.* That word is **device.** What word? *Signal.* **Device.** Spell **device.** *Signal.* **D-e-v-i-c-e.** What word did you spell? *Signal.* **Device.**
4. *Repeat step 3 for each remaining word in column 1.*
5. Now let's see if you remember all those words. Touch under the first word in column 1. *Pause.* What word? *Signal.* **Energy.**
6. Next word. *Pause.* What word? *Signal.* **Device.**
7. *Repeat step 6 for each remaining word in column 1.*
8. *Repeat the words in column 1 until firm.*

EXERCISE 2 Word practice

1. Everybody, touch column 2. *Check.* The letters **e-a** are in all those words. But be careful, because **e-a** makes different sounds in the words. Touch under the first word. *Pause.* What word? *Signal.* **Beam.**
2. Next word. *Pause.* What word? *Signal.* **Reaching.**
3. *Repeat step 2 for each remaining word in column 2.*
4. *Repeat the words in column 2 until firm.*

EXERCISE 3 Word practice

1. Everybody, touch column 3. *Check.* All those words end with the letters **e-d.** But be careful, because **e-d** makes different sounds in the words. Touch under the first word. *Pause.* What word? *Signal.* **Hollered.**
2. Next word. *Pause.* What word? *Signal.* **Crossed.**
3. *Repeat step 2 for each remaining word in column 3.*
4. *Repeat the words in column 3 until firm.*

EXERCISE 4 Word practice

1. Everybody, touch under the first word in column 4. *Pause.* What word? *Signal.* **Draw.**
2. Next word. *Pause.* What word? *Signal.* **Difficult.**
3. *Repeat step 2 for each remaining word in column 4.*
4. *Repeat the words in column 4 until firm.*
5. *Repeat steps 1–4 for column 5.*

EXERCISE 5 Vocabulary words

Task A
1. Everybody, touch column 6. *Check.* First you're going to read the words in column 6. Then we'll talk about what they mean.
2. Touch under the words in line 1. *Pause.* What words? *Signal.* **Sour face.**
3. Touch under the words in line 2. *Pause.* What words? *Signal.* **Save energy.**
4. Next word. *Pause.* What word? *Signal.* **Enter.**
5. *Repeat step 4 for each remaining word in column 6.*
6. *Repeat the words in column 6 until firm.*

Task B
1. Now let's talk about what those words mean. The words in line 1 are **sour face.** A **sour face** is the kind of face you would make after you just ate something sour, like a lemon.
2. Everybody, show me a sour-looking face. *Check.*

Task C
1. The words in line 2 are **save energy.** You learned what you do when you **save energy.**
2. Name some things you can do to save energy. *Call on individual students. Responses:* Ride a bus, turn off lights, etc.

Task D
1. Word 3 is **enter.** When you **enter** a place, you **go into** that place.
2. Everybody, what's another way of saying **She goes into the theater?** *Signal.* **She enters the theater.** *Repeat step 2 until firm.*
3. What's another way of saying **They went into the classroom?** *Signal.* **They entered the classroom.**

Task E
1. Word 4 is **solution.** The **solution** to a problem is the answer to the problem. Here's another way of saying **He found the answer to the problem: He found the solution to the problem.**
2. Your turn. What's another way of saying **He found the answer to the problem?** *Signal.* **He found the solution to the problem.**

EXERCISE 6 Individual test

1. Now I'm going to call on each of you to read a column of words. If you read all your words correctly, you will earn 2 points.
2. *Call on each student to read one column of words. Award points.*
3. Record your points in box WA.

After the students complete the word list activities, they read their *Textbook* stories aloud. The students must read the first part of each story within a specified decoding error limit. As the students read, the teacher presents comprehension questions at each circled letter. After the students complete their oral reading, they read the rest of the story silently. The teacher presents another group of comprehension questions at the end of the silent reading.

The comprehension questions in *Reading Mastery IV* emphasize reasoning skills and character analysis. In this sample lesson, the students evaluate problems and solutions, use rules to predict outcomes, interpret a character's feelings and motives, and predict a character's actions.

After the students finish the *Textbook* activities, they work independently in their *Workbooks* and *Skillbooks*. The independent work includes comprehension-passage items, story items, skill items, vocabulary items, and review items. In some lessons, the students play fact games and complete special projects.

In this sample lesson, the students complete story items and review items. The story items are based on the comprehension questions presented during the group reading. For the story items, the students recall narrative details, evaluate problems and solutions, and use rules to predict outcomes. The review items review previously taught facts. In this sample lesson, the students review facts they have learned about prehistoric eras and animal behavior.

B

·A Good Idea

The next evening, after supper, it happened. Leonard had no warning that it would happen. But it did. Everything in his mind suddenly came together and he had the idea for a great invention.Ⓐ

Here's how it happened: After supper, he went to his room to get a pencil. He was going to make some more drawings of ideas for inventions. When he started back to the kitchen, Grandmother Esther hollered at him, "Turn off the light in your room. Remember to save energy."

Leonard turned around, went back to his room, turned off the light, and stood there in the dark room. He felt the idea coming into his head. It got bigger and clearer and . . . "Hot dog!" he shouted.Ⓑ He shouted, "What an idea for an invention! Hot dog!" Ψ2 ERRORS Ψ He ran into the kitchen. "I've got it! What an idea! This is the best idea anybody ever had for an invention!"

His mother smiled. "I'll bet it's a machine that makes up a list of things you need at the store."Ⓒ

"Stop talking about that stupid machine," Grandmother Esther yelled from the other room. She ran into the kitchen. She was wearing her exercise outfit.Ⓓ Grandmother Esther asked, "What's your idea, Leonard?"

Leonard said, "Let me explain how it's going to work. It's dark outside. And it's dark in the living room of your house. But when you walk through the door to the living room, the light goes on automatically. The light stays on as long as you're in the living room. But when you leave the living room, the light goes off."Ⓔ

Leonard's mother shook her head. "That sounds far too difficult."

Grandmother Esther said, "It sounds difficult to you because you don't know how the electric eye works."Ⓕ

"The electric eye?" Leonard's mother asked.

Leonard said, "Here's how it works, Mom. There's a little beam of light that goes across the doorway to the living room. When you enter the room, you break the beam. When you break that beam, the light turns on. Then when you leave the room, you break the beam and the light goes off."

EXERCISE 7   Reading: decoding

1. Everybody, find part B in your textbook. *Wait. Call on a student.* What's the error limit for this story? **9 errors.**
2. *Call on individual students to read two or three sentences, starting with the title.*

Comprehension tasks

Ⓐ *Call on a student.* What happened that evening?
  Idea: Leonard got an idea for a great invention.
  • Everybody, did Leonard know that this would happen? *Signal.* **No.**
Ⓑ *Call on a student.* Why did he shout?
  Idea: He was excited.
  • *Call on a student.* How did he feel?
  Ideas: Happy; excited.
Ⓒ Everybody, do you think Leonard's getting tired of hearing about that machine? *Signal.* **Yes.**
Ⓓ *Call on a student.* Look at the picture. What is Grandmother Esther wearing? *Idea:* Her exercise outfit.
Ⓔ Leonard explained how the invention would work. Listen to that part again.
  Read from Ⓓ *to* Ⓔ.
  • *Call on a student.* What happens when you walk **into** the room? *Idea:* The light goes on.
  • *Call on a student.* What happens when you **leave** the room? *Idea:* The light goes off.
  • *Call on a student.* What kind of thing could make the lights go on and off automatically?
  Idea: An electric eye.
Ⓕ Everybody, did Grandmother Esther know how Leonard was thinking of making the lights go on and off? *Signal.* **Yes.**
  • Everybody, what was he going to use? *Signal.* **An electric eye.**

"Oh, my," Leonard's mother said. He could tell from her tone of voice that she didn't understand what he said.

"Good thinking," Grandmother Esther said, and slapped Leonard on the back. "That's a fine idea for an invention, a fine idea."

"Thank you," Leonard said. 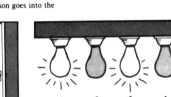(G)

Grandmother Esther made a sour-looking face. Slowly she said, "There's one big problem with being a good inventor. You have to think of all the things that could go wrong."

"What could go wrong?" Leonard asked.

Grandmother Esther explained. "When you break the beam one time, the light goes on. When you break the beam the next time, the light goes off. When you break the beam the next time, the light goes on."

"Right," Leonard said.

"That's the problem," Grandmother Esther said. "What if two people walk into a dark room? When the first one goes into the room, the light will go on. Now the second person goes into the

room. What happens to the light?"

"It goes off," Leonard said very sadly. He shook his head. "Now both people are in the dark, and my invention stinks." (H) ᛐ **9 ERRORS** ᛐ

"Wrong!" Grandmother Esther shouted. "Both people are in the dark, but your invention does not stink. Every invention has problems. An inventor has to look at these problems and try to solve them. But you must remember that inventing something is more than just getting an idea. You must work on that idea until it is a good idea. Then you must take that good idea and make it into a good invention. Just because there's a problem doesn't mean that you give up. You've got a great idea."

Leonard's mother said, "I have a great idea for an invention. It's a machine that . . ."

"Not now," Grandmother Esther said. "We're close to a real invention."

Leonard said, "I'll just have to think about the problem and try to figure out how to solve it."

(G) Earlier, Grandmother Esther had said that she didn't think Leonard had the right idea for an invention. Everybody, do you think she feels that the electric eye invention is the right idea? *Signal.* **Yes.**

(H) Everybody, is that the way Leonard wants it to work? *Signal.* **No.**

● Read the rest of the story to yourselves and be ready to answer some questions. Remember, Leonard has just said that he thinks his invention stinks. Raise your hand when you're done.

● *After all students have raised their hands:*

● Everybody, is Leonard going to give up? *Signal.* **No.**

● *Call on a student.* What is he going to do? *Idea:* Think about the problem and try to solve it.

● Everybody, look at the picture. The picture shows Leonard's invention. The lights in the box show what will happen each time the beam of light is broken. When we start out, the light is **not on.** Everybody, so what will happen when the beam is broken **one time?** *Signal.* **The light will go on.**

Lesson 46

A

Story items

1. Leonard got his idea for a great invention when Grandmother Esther told him to do something. What did she tell him to do? _____

2. At first, what did Leonard's mother think his idea was?

3. **Answer these questions about Leonard's invention:**
   a. What does the light in the room do when you walk into the room?

   b. What does the light do when you leave the room?

4. What will Leonard use to make the lights work automatically?

5. Did Leonard's mother understand how his invention would work?

6. a. Grandmother Esther told Leonard that every invention has

   b. So what does the inventor have to do?

7. Leonard's invention has problems. Let's say two people walk into a room.
   a. What happens to the light in the room when the first person enters?

   b. What happens to the light when the second person enters?

8. Here's the rule about an electric eye. **Each time the beam of light is broken, the light changes.** Color the correct bulbs for each problem. The first problem is already done for you.

   a. The beam is broken 4 times. Is the light **on** or **off** at the end?

   b. Here's another problem.

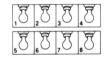

   The beam is broken 8 times. Color the bulbs. Is the light **on** or **off** at the end?

   c. Here's another problem.

   The beam is broken 3 times. Color the bulbs. Is the light **on** or **off** at the end?

Lesson 46

Number your paper from 1 through 17.

Review items

● Answer these questions about an electric eye on a shop door:

1. When somebody walks in the door, their body stops the beam of light from reaching the _____

2. When their body stops the beam, what happens?

3. What does that tell the shopkeeper?

4. Who had more things made by humans—**people who lived in caves** or **people who live today?**

5. What kind of animals lived in the Mesozoic era?

6. What kind of animals live in the Cenozoic era?

7. What kinds of animals lived in the Paleozoic era?

8. Name a dinosaur that could fight with Tyrannosaurus.

9. The first thing you do when you think like an inventor is find a _____.

10. What's the next thing you do?

● Look at the footprints.

11. Write the letter of the footprint made by the heaviest animal.

12. Write the letter of the footprint made by the lightest animal.

13. In the summer, the place where Oomoo lives changes in three ways. The seals and walruses _____

14. The snow _____

15. The killer whales _____

J   F   K

Reading Mastery V

Reading Mastery V contains 120 daily lessons that emphasize literary analysis and extended writing. Students in the program read a wide range of classic and modern fiction and prose, including two full-length novels, and they learn how to analyze characters, settings, plots, and themes. The daily writing assignments focus on the meaning of literature and encourage students to think critically. Other program activities include making outlines, inferring word meaning from context, and interpreting reference materials.

Materials

For the teacher:

*   *Presentation Books* (2)
*   *Teacher's Guide*

For the students:

*   *Textbook*
*   *Skillbook*
*   *Workbook*

The *Textbook* contains both classic and modern literature. Students read two full-length novels, as well as short stories, comprehension passages, factual articles, biographies, and poetry. Here is a partial listing of the *Textbook* contents.

*   **The Wizard of Oz** - L. Frank Baum's classic novel about Dorothy's search for the wonderful Wizard.
*   **The Prince and the Pauper** - The famous novel about an identity switch between a prince and a pauper, by Samuel Clemens.
*   **Buck** and **Brown Wolf** - Two Jack London stories about sled dogs and the Yukon gold rush.
*   **The Miraculous Pitcher** and **The Golden Touch** - Two of Nathaniel Hawthorne's superb retellings of the Greek myths.
*   **Jackie Robinson** and **Jane Addams** - Biographies of famous Americans.
*   **The Secret Cave, A Horse to Remember**, and **Adventure on the Rocky Ridge** - Contemporary stories written especially for the program.

*   **The Ugly Duckling, The Beauty and the Beast, The Cat That Walked by Himself**, and **Dick Whittington** - Classic folk and fairy tales by Andersen, d'Aulnoy, Kipling, and Lang.
*   **Open Range, Trees, In Time of Silver Rain**, and **The Spider and the Fly** – Lyric and narrative poems by Jackson, Behn, Hughes, and Howitt.
*   **Comprehension Passages** - Short passages that provide background information for the stories.
*   **Factual Articles** - Articles about people and the world.

Sample Activities

The following activities appear in lesson 77 in *Reading Mastery V*.

The students begin lesson 77 — and every lesson — by reading word lists. There are four types: lists of words that are difficult to decode; lists of words with common features; lists of words that are easy to decode; and lists of vocabulary words.

First the students read the lists in unison; then they complete exercises with the vocabulary words. The vocabulary exercises take several forms. In exercise 4, for example, the teacher explains the meanings of one list of vocabulary words, and then the students practice using the words in context. In exercise 5, the students read sentences that contain new vocabulary words. The students must then infer word meaning from context. Later in the program, the students read the meanings of new vocabulary words.

PART A Word Lists			PART B Vocabulary Sentences
1 linen frenzy appetite credit woven dispair pity secure	**2** precious delicious anxious spacious	**3** flexible convenient inconvenient accompany accompanied	1. She was very unhappy about a lot of things, but she was most <u>discontented</u> about the mess that was in the basement. 2. When he started eating he had a huge <u>appetite</u>, but when he finished the main part of the meal, he had no room for dessert. 3. He didn't want anybody to steal his treasure, so he looked for a <u>secure</u> place. 4. The little boy was so poor, sad, and cold that I felt great <u>pity</u> for him.
4 **Vocabulary words** 1. deserve credit 2. linen 3. frenzy 4. occupied	**5** **Vocabulary words** 1. discontent 2. appetite 3. secure 4. pity		

EXERCISE 1 Word practice

1. Everybody, find lesson 77, part A in your skillbook. *Wait.* Touch under each word in column 1 as I read it.
2. The first word is **linen.**
3. Next word. **Frenzy.**
4. *Repeat step 3 for each remaining word in column 1.*
5. Your turn. Read the first word. *Signal.* **Linen.**
6. Next word. *Signal.* **Frenzy.**
7. *Repeat step 6 for each remaining word in column 1.*
8. *Repeat the words in column 1 until firm.*

EXERCISE 2 Word family

1. Everybody, touch column 2. *Check.*
   All those words end with the letters **i-o-u-s.**
   Touch under the first word. *Pause.*
   What word? *Signal.* **Precious.**
2. Next word. *Pause.* What word? *Signal.*
   Delicious.
3. *Repeat step 2 for each remaining word in column 2.*
4. *Repeat the words in column 2 until firm.*

EXERCISE 3 Word practice

1. Everybody, touch under the first word in column 3. *Pause.* What word? *Signal.* **Flexible.**
2. Next word. *Pause.* What word? *Signal.*
   Convenient.
3. *Repeat step 2 for each remaining word in column 3.*
4. *Repeat the words in column 3 until firm.*

EXERCISE 4 Vocabulary development

Task A

1. Everybody, touch column 4. *Check.*
   First you're going to read the words in column 4. Then we'll talk about what they mean.
2. Touch under the first line. *Pause.*
   What words? *Signal.* **Deserve credit.**
3. Next word. *Pause.*
   What word? *Signal.* **Linen.**
4. *Repeat step 3 for each remaining word in column 4.*
5. *Repeat the words in column 4 until firm.*

Task B

   Now let's talk about what those words mean.
   The words in line 1 are **deserve credit.** When you succeed in doing something, you **deserved credit** for doing that thing. Here's another way of saying **She succeeded at solving the problem: She deserved credit for solving the problem.**
   Everybody, what's another way of saying **She succeeded at solving the problem?** *Signal.* **She deserved credit for solving the problem.**

Task C

   Word 2 is **linen. Linen** is an expensive cloth that some sheets and dresses are made of. Everybody, what's an expensive cloth that some sheets and dresses are made of? *Signal.* **Linen.**

Task D

1. Word 3 is **frenzy.** When you do things in a very hurried and excited way, you do them in a **frenzy.** Here's another way of saying **She ran around in excitement: She ran around in a frenzy?** Everybody, what's another way of saying **She ran around in excitement?** *Signal.* **She ran around in a frenzy.**
2. Everybody, what's another way of saying **They cooked the dinner in a hurry?** *Signal.* **They cooked the dinner in a frenzy.**

Task E

1. Word 4 is **occupied.** When you are **occupied** with something, you are busy with that thing. Here's another way of saying **You are busy with your thoughts: You are occupied with your thoughts.**
2. Everybody, what's another way of saying **She was busy with the customer?** *Signal.* **She was occupied with the customer.**
3. Everybody, what's another way of saying **They were busy with the details of the problem?** *Signal.* **They were occupied with the details of the problem.**

EXERCISE 5 Vocabulary from context

Task A

1. Everybody, touch column 5. *Check.*
   First you're going to read the words in column 5. Then we'll talk about what they mean.
2. Touch under the first word. *Pause.*
   What word? *Signal.* **Discontent.**
3. Next word. *Pause.* What word? *Signal.* **Appetite.**
4. *Repeat step 3 for each remaining word in column 5.*
5. *Repeat the words in column 5 until firm.*

Task B

1. Everybody, find part B in your skillbook. *Check.* I'll read those sentences. You figure out what the underlined part in each sentence means.
2. Sentence one. She was very unhappy about a lot of things, but she was most underlined discontented about the mess that was in the basement.
   Call on a student. What could **discontented** mean? *Idea:* Dissatisfied.
3. *Repeat step 2 for each remaining sentence.*
   Answer Key: **2.** *Idea:* Desire for food.
         3. *Idea:* Safe.
         4. *Idea:* Sorrow.

After the students complete the word list activities, they read aloud from their *Textbooks*. The students read the first part of each story within a specified decoding error limit. As the students read, the teacher presents comprehension questions at each circled letter. After the students complete their oral reading, they read the rest of the story silently. The amount of silent reading increases as the program progresses. The teacher presents another group of comprehension questions at the end of the silent reading.

The comprehension questions in *Reading Mastery V* stress literary skills and interpretive comprehension. In this sample lesson, the students predict outcomes, analyze settings, and analyze a character's actions, motives, and point of view.

After the students finish the *Textbook* activities, they work independently in their *Workbooks* and *Skillbooks*. The independent work includes skill items, story items, review items, vocabulary items, and writing assignments.

The skill items teach important comprehension and study skills, such as inferring the main idea, interpreting maps, and using glossaries. In this sample lesson, the students read a passage and then write the main idea of the passage. In later lessons, the students list the supporting details for a main idea.

The story items present questions about the day's story. In this sample lesson, the students sequence narrative events, infer causes and effects, and analyze characters.

The review items review previously taught skills. In this sample lesson, the students review facts they have learned about dog breeds, story characters, and Greek gods. They also place events on a time-line. Finally, they review vocabulary words by placing them in sentence context.

The last independent work activity is the writing assignment. This assignment is designed to improve the students' writing skills. The students write several sentences on a topic that relates to their *Textbook* stories.

The Golden Touch

PART 2Ⓐ

The stranger gazed about the room, and when his glowing smile had shone upon all the golden objects that were there, he turned again to Midas.

"You are a wealthy man, friend Midas," he observed. "I doubt whether any other four walls on earth contain so much gold as this room contains."

"I have done pretty well—pretty well," answered Midas in a discontented tone. "But, after all, it is a very small amount, when you consider that it has taken me my whole life to get it together."Ⓑ Midas continued, "If one could live a thousand years, he might have time to grow rich."

"What?" exclaimed the stranger. "Then you are not satisfied?"

Midas shook his head.

"And what would satisfy you?" asked the stranger. "I would like to know."

Midas paused. He felt that this stranger had the power to grant any wish. He had only to speak and obtain whatever he might want. So he thought, and thought, and thought. His imagination heaped up one golden mountain after another. But he was unable to imagine mountains that were big enough. At last, a bright idea occurred to King Midas. It seemed really as bright as the glistening metal which he loved so much.

Raising his head, he looked the stranger in the face.

The visitor observed, "Well, Midas, I see that you have at last hit upon something that will satisfy you. Tell me your wish."Ⓒ

"It is only this," replied Midas. "I am weary of collecting my treasures with so much trouble, and seeing the heap so small after I have done my best. I wish everything that I touch could be changed to gold!"

"The Golden Touch!" exclaimed the stranger. "You certainly deserve credit, friend Midas, for having such a brilliant idea. But are you quite sure that this will satisfy you?"

"How could it fail?" said Midas.

"And you will never regret having it?"

"What could make me regret it?" asked Midas. "I need nothing else to make me perfectly happy."Ⓓ ★6 ERRORS★

"You shall have your wish," replied the stranger, waving his hand in farewell. "Tomorrow, at sunrise, you will find yourself gifted with the Golden Touch."

The stranger then became so terribly bright that Midas closed his eyes. When he opened them again he saw only one yellow sunbeam in the room. All around him was the glistening of the precious metal which he had spent his life collecting.

Midas did not sleep well that night. His mind was like the mind of a child who had been promised a new plaything in the morning. Day had hardly peeped over the hills when King Midas was wide awake. He stretched his arms out of bed and began to touch objects that were within reach. He was anxious to prove whether the Golden Touch had really come, according to the stranger's promise.

Midas laid his finger on a chair by the bedside, and on other things, but he was very disappointed to find that they remained exactly the same as before. He was afraid that he had only dreamed about the stranger, or else that the stranger had been making fun of him. And how miserable it would be if Midas had to be content with the little gold he could scrape together by ordinary means, instead of creating gold by a touch.

All this happened while it was only the gray of the morning, with only a streak of

---

EXERCISE 6   Decoding and comprehension

1. Everybody, turn to page 292 in your textbook. *Wait. Call on a student.* What's the error limit for this lesson? **6 errors.**

2. *Call on individual students to read. Present the tasks specified for each circled letter.*

Ⓐ Where was Midas at the end of the last part? *Idea:* In his treasure room.
- Who was with him? **A stranger.**
- What did Midas think this stranger was? **A god.**
- Why did Midas think this god had paid him a visit? *Idea:* To grant him a favor.

Ⓑ Did Midas think that he had enough gold? **No.**

Ⓒ If you think about the title of this story, you'll know what Midas will wish for. What is that? *Idea:* The golden touch.
- How would a golden touch work? *Idea:* Everything you touch turns into gold.

Ⓓ Is Midas thinking clearly? **No.**
- Name some problems that you might have if everything you touched turned into gold. *Response:* Student preference.
- Read the rest of the story to yourselves and be ready to answer some questions.

After all students have finished reading:
- How well did Midas sleep that night? *Idea:* Not very well.

brightness along the edge of the sky. Midas was in a very bad mood. He kept growing sadder and sadder, until the earliest sunbeam shone through the window and lit up the ceiling over his head. It seemed to Midas that this bright yellow sunbeam reflected in an unusual way on the white covering of the bed. Looking more closely, he was astonished and delighted to find that this linen cloth had been changed into woven gold, the purest and brightest he had ever seen! The Golden Touch had come to him with the first sunbeam!

Midas started up in a kind of joyful frenzy, and ran about the room grasping at everything that happened to be in his way. He seized one of the bedposts, and it immediately became a golden pillar. He pulled open a window curtain, and the cord grew heavy in his hand—a mass of gold. Midas took up a book from the table. At his first touch, the cover became solid gold. And when he ran his fingers through the pages, the book became a bundle of thin, gold plates, and all the wise words in the book disappeared.

Midas quickly put on his clothes, and was overjoyed to see himself in a magnificent suit of gold cloth, which was flexible and soft, although it was very, very heavy. He drew out his handkerchief, which little Marygold had made for him. That was also gold.

Somehow or other this last change did not quite please King Midas. He would have rather had his little daughter's handkerchief remain just as it was when she climbed upon his knee and put it into his hand.

But it was not worthwhile to worry about a handkerchief. Midas now took his spectacles from his pocket and put them on his nose to see more clearly. But he discovered that he could not possibly see through them, for the glass had turned into a plate of yellow metal. They were worthless as spectacles, but valuable as gold. It seemed rather inconvenient to Midas that, with all his wealth, he could never again be rich enough to own a pair of usable spectacles.

"It is no great problem," he said to himself. "Every great good is accompanied by some small inconvenience. The Golden Touch is worth the loss of a pair of spectacles. My own eyes will serve for ordinary purposes, and little Marygold will soon be old enough to read to me."

Wise King Midas was so excited by his good fortune that the palace did not seem large enough for him. He therefore went downstairs, and smiled when he observed that the handrail of the staircase became a bar of gold as his hand passed over it. He lifted the door latch. It was brass only a moment ago, but it became golden when his fingers left it. He went into the garden, where he found a great number of beautiful roses in full bloom, and others in all the stages of lovely bud and blossom. Their fragrance was very delicious in the morning breeze.

But Midas knew a way to make them far more precious, to his way of thinking. So he went from bush to bush, and used his magic touch until every flower and bud was changed to gold. By the time this work was completed, King Midas was called to breakfast. The morning air had given him an excellent appetite, and he quickly returned to the palace.

- Did Midas get up in the morning **before** sunrise or **after** sunrise? **Before sunrise.**
- When did Midas notice that he had the golden touch? *Idea:* When the first sunbeam came into his room.
- What was the first thing that had been changed into gold? *Idea:* The bed covering.
- What happened to the book that he touched? *Idea:* It turned into gold.
- What was lost when the book changed into gold? *Idea:* All the wise words.
- What was the problem with his spectacles? *Idea:* He couldn't see through them.
- How did Midas plan to solve the problem of not being able to see clearly? *Idea:* Have Marygold help him.
- What did he do in the garden? *Idea:* Turned all the roses into gold.
- Why did he return to the palace at the end of this part? *Idea:* He was called for breakfast.
- What do you think is going to happen when he tries to eat breakfast? *Response:* Student preference.

Award 4 points or have the students reread to the error limit sign.

Lesson 77

R	W	B	T

Story Items

1. Put the following events in the right order by numbering them from 1 through 4.

_____ Midas turned a book to gold.

_____ Midas turned a rose to gold.

_____ Midas asked the stranger for a favor.

_____ Midas had a hard time sleeping.

Review Items

2. Write which god each picture shows. Choose from **Apollo, Hermes, Poseidon** or **Zeus.**

a. _____

b. _____

c. _____

d. _____

3. Here are some events from Jackie Robinson's life.
   - Jackie leaves UCLA
   - Jackie dies
   - Jackie helps win the World Series
   - Jackie first plays for the Dodgers

Write the correct event after each date on the time line.

1972 _____
      _____

1955 _____
      _____

1947 _____
      _____

1941 _____
      _____

PART C Main Idea Paragraphs

Read the paragraph below. Then write a sentence that tells the main idea.

1. Baucis and Philemon lived in a small cottage outside a village. They did not have much money or food, but they were happy. Sometimes, they would see a stranger walking up the path to their cottage. At those times, Baucis would hurry into the house to make dinner and Philemon would greet the stranger. Then Baucis and Philemon would give the stranger some dinner and do everything they could to make the stranger comfortable. After dinner, they would give up their bed to the stranger and sleep on the floor.

PART D Story Items

2. a. Before the stranger came to his room, was Midas satisfied with the wealth he had?
   b. Why didn't Midas just ask for a mountain of gold?
   c. What did Midas ask the stranger for?
   d. Did Midas think he would ever regret that gift?
3. Midas woke up early the next morning.
   a. Did the golden touch work at first?
   b. When did the golden touch begin to work?
   c. What was the first object that changed into gold?
   d. After Midas touched the book, what couldn't he do with that book?
4. a. When Midas put on his clothes, what was different about their weight?
   b. Write the name of the first object that disturbed Midas when it changed to gold.
   c. Who had made that object for Midas?
5. a. What kind of flowers did Midas touch?
   b. How did the flowers smell before he touched them?

PART E Review Items

6. Write which breed of dog each statement describes.
   a. This is the fastest breed.
   b. This breed is good at herding.
   c. This breed has an excellent nose.
   d. This may be the smartest breed.
   e. This breed is very brave.
7. Write which character could have made each statement. Choose from the **Lion,** the **Cat that Walked,** or the **Ugly Duckling.**
   a. "I am the king of beasts."
   b. "I live with people, but they can't tell me what to do."
   c. "I used to be a coward."
   d. "I finally saw myself when I looked in the water."
8. Use the words in the box to fill in the blanks or replace the underlined words.

disagreeable	insulted	rookie
astonishment	contract	beat
main job	a lot of	spacious
in disguise	inhabitants	

   a. The rainy weather was very _____ to Sidney.
   b. Cora decided to go to a school that would prepare her for a new career.
   c. She didn't want to perform in the play, but she had a _____ that said she had to.
   d. At the Halloween party, Mary was _____ as a bear.
   e. They were surprised and full of amazement.
   f. Most of the _____ of the town chased the frogs into the lake.

PART F Writing Assignment

Write at least **four** sentences about the problems you might have if you had the golden touch.

Reading Mastery VI

Reading Mastery VI contains 120 daily lessons that focus on literary language, reasoning strategies, and extended writing. The reading selections include novels, short stories, poems, factual articles, biographies, and plays. Students in the program learn how to interpret complex sentence forms, figurative language, and literary irony; they also learn how to identify contradictions and rebut faulty logic. In addition, students write complete paragraphs on issues related to the reading selections, as well as short stories and poems of their own.

Materials

For the teacher:

- *Presentation Books* (2)
- *Teacher's Guide*

For the students:

- *Textbook*
- *Workbook*
- *Skillbook*

The *Textbook* contains both classic and modern literature. Students read a full-length novel and three novellas, as well as short stories, a play, poetry, a biography, comprehension passages, and factual articles. Here is a partial listing of the *Textbook* contents:

- **Tom Sawyer** - Mark Twain's classic novel about growing up on the Mississippi River.
- **The Odyssey** - A prose translation of Homer's epic poem.
- **Sara Crewe** - A romantic novella about a girl in a boarding school, by Frances Burnett.
- **The Cruise of the Dazzler** - A novella about pirates, by Jack London.
- **The Doughnuts** and **Mystery Yarn** - Two hilarious stories about Homer Price, by Robert McCloskey.
- **The Spider, the Cave and the Pottery Bowl** - A modern story about an Indian girl, by Eleanor Clymer.
- **The Last Leaf, Persephone, The Necklace, A White Heron**, and **The Star** - Classic short stories by O. Henry, Nathaniel Hawthorne, Guy de Maupassant, Sarah Orne Jewett, and H.G. Wells.

- **The Tide Rises, the Tide Falls, Written in March, Casey at the Bat**, and **Miracles** - Classic poems by Henry Wadsworth Longfellow, William Wordsworth, Ernest Thayer, and Walt Whitman.
- **Harriet Tubman** - A biography of the famous guide on the Underground Railroad.
- **All in Favor** - A contemporary play about a children's club.
- **Comprehension Passages** - Short passages that provide background information for the stories.
- **Factual articles** - Articles about people and the world.

Sample Activities

The following activities appear in lesson 47 of *Reading Mastery VI*.

The students begin lesson 47 — and every lesson — by reading word lists. There are three types: lists of words that are difficult to decode, lists of words that are easy to decode, and lists of vocabulary words. Many lessons contain only one or two types of lists.

First the students read the lists in unison; then they complete vocabulary exercises. There are two basic types of vocabulary exercises: an introductory exercise and a review exercise. Part B is an introductory exercise. The students read the meanings of the new vocabulary words and then practice using the words in context. Part C is a review exercise. The students read words they have already learned. Then they use those words to complete sentences.

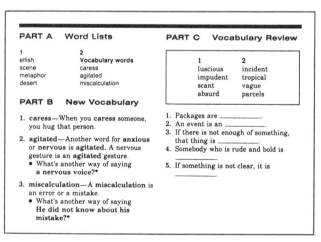

EXERCISE 1 Word practice

1. Everybody, find lesson 47, part A in your skillbook. *Wait.* Touch under the first word in column 1. *Pause.* What word? *Signal.* **Elfish.**
2. Next Word. *Pause.* What word? *Signal.* **Scene.**
3. *Repeat step 2 for each remaining word in column 1.*
4. *Repeat the words in column 1 until firm.*

EXERCISE 2 Vocabulary development

Task A

1. Everybody, touch column 2.
First you're going to read the words in column 2. Then you're going to read about what they mean.
2. Read the first word. *Signal.* **Caress.**
3. Next word. *Signal.* **Agitated.**
4. *Repeat step 3 for each remaining word in column 2.*
5. *Repeat the words in column 2 until firm.*

Task B

1. Everybody, look at part B. You're going to read this part out loud.
2. *Call on individual students to read each item aloud.*
   - *For questions followed by an asterisk, say:* "Everybody, what's the answer?"
   - *For questions without an asterisk, call on one student and say:* "What's the answer?"

Key: **2. An agitated voice.**
     3. He did not know about his miscalculation

EXERCISE 3 Vocabulary review

1. Everybody, look at part C. The words in the box are words you've learned.
2. Read the first word. *Signal.* **Luscious.**
3. Next. *Signal.* **Impudent.**
4. *Repeat step 3 for the remaining words in the box.*
5. *Repeat the words in the box until firm.*
6. I'll read the items. When I come to a blank, everybody say the part that goes in the blank.
7. Look over item 1. *Pause.* Listen. Packages are *Pause. Signal.* **parcels.**
8. *Repeat step 7 for each remaining item.*

Key: **2. incident**
     3. scant
     4. impudent
     5. vague

After the students complete the word list activities, they go over new skill exercises with the teacher. These skill exercises teach a variety of comprehension, literary, and reference skills. For example, the students learn how to identify contradictions and logical fallacies, how to interpret anaphora and apposition, and how to use reference materials.

In this sample lesson, the students learn how to write similes. Individual students read the exercise, and the teacher presents questions at each circled letter. Later in the lesson, the students will write the answers for the exercise.

PART D Similes

Here's how to make up a simile. You start with an accurate statement such as: *Her eyes were blue.* Next, you name something that could be as blue as her eyes.Ⓐ

Here's a simile that tells what her eyes were like: *Her eyes were like a cloudless sky.*Ⓑ
1. Make up a simile for this accurate statement: *The man ran fast.*
   a. Name something that is fast.Ⓒ
   b. Make up a simile that tells how the man ran. Use the word **like** in your simile.Ⓓ
2. Make up a simile for this accurate statement: *The woman was very strong.*
   a. Name something that is strong.
   b. Make up a simile that tells how strong the woman was. Use the word **like** in your simile.

EXERCISE 4 Figurative language: similes

1. Everybody, look at part D. *Check.*
2. *Call on individual students to read. Present the tasks specified for each circled letter.*
Ⓐ Name something that could be as blue as her eyes. *Idea:* A cloudless sky.
Ⓑ Say the simile about her eyes. **Her eyes were like a cloudless sky.**
   - What color is a cloudless sky? Blue.
   - What color are her eyes? Blue.
Ⓒ *Call on individual students.* Name something. *Ideas:* Wind, bullet, rocket, deer.
   - You will use that word in the simile.
Ⓓ Say the simile. *Ideas:* The man ran like the wind, a bullet, a rocket, a deer.
   - You'll write the answers for both items later.

After the students go over the skill exercise, they read in their *Textbooks*. Most *Textbook* lessons begin with a group of *Find-outs* that the students read aloud. The *Find-outs* alert the students to important elements of the story they are about to read. Later in the lesson, the students will answer questions that are based on the *Find-outs*.

As soon as the students finish reading the *Find-outs*, they usually read the rest of the *Textbook* lesson silently. The students read almost all of the *Textbook* novels and stories silently; however, they continue to read the poems, plays, and factual articles aloud.

When the students have finished their silent reading, the teacher presents comprehension questions about the reading. These questions stress literary skills and interpretive comprehension. In this sample lesson, the students recall narrative events, infer a character's motives, and identify perspectives.

EXERCISE 5 Story reading

1. Everybody, turn to page 160 in your textbook.
2. *Call on individual students to read the title and the find-outs aloud. Then tell the students to read the chapter to themselves.*

After all students have finished reading:

- Which animal did Sara find in her room? **The monkey.**
- Where did Sara take the animal? *Ideas:* Home; to the Indian Gentleman.
- The Indian Gentleman began to ask Sara some questions. Who had first taken Sara to the school? *Ideas:* Her father; Captain Crewe.
- What had happened to Captain Crewe's money? *Idea:* It had been lost.
- Then what had happened to Captain Crewe? *Idea:* He died.
- Who do you think the friend is who was responsible for Captain Crewe's misfortune? *Idea:* Student preference.

CHAPTER 12

The Monkey

Find out:
- *Which animal Sara found in her room.*
- *Whose house Sara went to.*
- *Which character Sara finally met.*
- *What that character told Sara.*

On the night that Sara received the parcels, she carried out a plan she had been thinking about for some time. She wrote this note to her unknown friend:

> I want to thank you for being so kind to me—so beautifully kind, and making everything like a fairy story. I am so grateful to you and I am so happy! I used to be so lonely and cold and hungry, and now, just think what you have done for me! Thank you—thank you—thank you!
> THE GIRL IN THE ATTIC

The next morning, she left this note on the little table, and it was taken away with the other things, so she felt sure the magician had received it.

A few nights later, a very odd thing happened. She found something in the room which she certainly would never have expected. When she came in as usual she saw something small and dark in her chair—an odd, tiny figure, which turned a small and weird-looking face toward her.

"Why, it's the monkey!" Sara cried. "It is the Indian Gentleman's monkey!"

It *was* the monkey, sitting up and looking forlorn. Very soon, Sara found out how he had gotten into her room. The skylight was open, and it was easy to guess that he had crept out of his master's garret window, which was only a few feet away. The monkey had probably been attracted by the light in Sara's attic, and had crept in. And there he was. And when Sara went to him, he actually put out his queer, elfish little hands, caught her dress, and jumped into her arms.

"Oh, you poor little thing!" said Sara, caressing him. "I can't help liking you, but you have such a forlorn look on your little face."

The monkey sat and looked at her while she talked and seemed much interested in her remarks, if one could judge by his eyes and his forehead, and the way he moved his head up and down. The monkey held his head sideways and scratched it with his little hand. He examined Sara quite

seriously, and anxiously, too. The monkey felt the material of her dress, touched her hands, climbed up and examined her ears, and then sat on her shoulder holding a lock of her hair, looking mournful but not at all agitated. Upon the whole, the monkey seemed pleased with Sara.

"But I must take you back," she said to the monkey, "though I'm sorry to have to do it. Oh, you *would* be good company!"

She lifted the monkey from her shoulder, set him on her knee, and gave him a bit of cake. He sat and nibbled it, and then put his head on one side, looked at her, wrinkled his forehead, and then nibbled again.

"But you must go home," said Sara at last, and she took the monkey in her arms to carry him downstairs. Evidently he did not want to leave the room, for as they reached the door he clung to her neck and gave a little scream of anger.

"You mustn't be an ungrateful monkey," said Sara. "You ought to be fond of your own family. I am sure your master is good to you."

Nobody saw Sara on her way out, and very soon she was standing on the Indian Gentleman's front steps, and the Lascar had opened the door for her.

"I found your monkey in my room," she said in Indian. "I think he got in through the window."

The man began a rapid outpouring of thanks, but he was interrupted by an agitated and hollow voice that came through the open door of the nearest room. The instant he heard it, the Lascar disappeared and left Sara in the front hall, still holding the monkey.

It was not many moments, however, before the Lascar came back bringing a message. His master had told him to bring Sara into the library. The master was very ill, but he wished to see Sara.

Sara followed the Lascar. When she entered the room the Indian Gentleman was lying on an easy chair, propped up with pillows. He looked frightfully ill. His pale face was thin, and his eyes were hollow. He gave Sara a rather curious look.

After the students finish the *Textbook* activities, they work independently in their *Workbooks* and *Skillbooks*. The independent work includes skill items, story items, review items, vocabulary items, and writing assignments.

For the skill items in this sample lesson, the students interpret maps, identify relevant evidence, and analyze exaggerations. The skill items often involve characters and events from the *Textbook* stories. In this sample lesson, the map task reviews events from *The Odyssey*, while the relevant-information task involves characters from *Sara Crewe*. This constant use of story material helps to make the stories more meaningful to the students.

The story items present questions about the day's story. Many of these questions are based on the *Find-outs* and on the comprehension questions that the teacher presents orally. In this sample lesson, the students recall narrative events, predict outcomes, interpret a character's feelings, and identify a character's traits.

The vocabulary items review the vocabulary words that the students have learned. The students use context clues to complete sentences with the vocabulary words.

The last independent work activity is the writing assignment. The students not only write paragraphs on assigned topics, but also write stories and poems of their own. In this lesson, the students write a story that relates to the novella *Sara Crewe*.

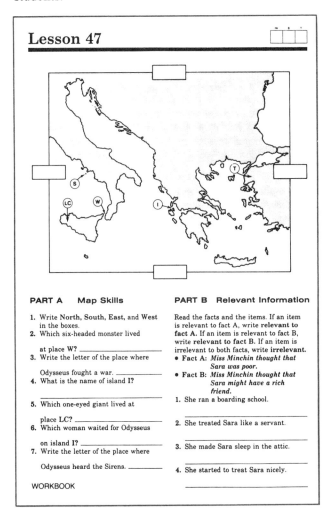

Lesson 47

PART A   Map Skills

1. Write North, South, East, and West in the boxes.
2. Which six-headed monster lived at place W? _____
3. Write the letter of the place where Odysseus fought a war. _____
4. What is the name of island I? _____
5. Which one-eyed giant lived at place LC? _____
6. Which woman waited for Odysseus on island I? _____
7. Write the letter of the place where Odysseus heard the Sirens. _____

WORKBOOK

PART B   Relevant Information

Read the facts and the items. If an item is relevant to fact A, write **relevant to fact A**. If an item is relevant to fact B, write **relevant to fact B**. If an item is irrelevant to both facts, write **irrelevant**.
• Fact A: *Miss Minchin thought that Sara was poor.*
• Fact B: *Miss Minchin thought that Sara might have a rich friend.*

1. She ran a boarding school.

_____

2. She treated Sara like a servant.

_____

3. She made Sara sleep in the attic.

_____

4. She started to treat Sara nicely.

_____

Lesson 47

PART E   Story Items

1. a. Why did Sara write a note?
   b. Which animal did Sara find in her room a few nights later?
   c. What had that animal crawled through to get into Sara's room?
   d. Where did Sara take that animal?
2. a. The Indian Gentleman's face was

   • pale   • red   • blue
   b. How did the Indian Gentleman seem to feel?
      • Content   • Ill   • Smug
3. The Indian Gentleman began to ask Sara some questions.
   a. Who had first taken her to the school?
   b. What had happened to her father's money?
   c. Then what happened to Sara's father?
   d. Who do you think the friend is who was responsible for her father's misfortune?
   e. What could the Indian Gentleman do for Sara?
4. At the end of the chapter the Indian Gentleman said, "Tell Carmichael that I have found the child."
   a. Which child was he referring to?
   b. What do you think the Indian Gentleman intends to do for that child?
5. Write which character each statement describes. Choose from the **Indian Gentleman**, **Captain Crewe**, **Sara**, or the **Lascar**.
   a. This character thought that all his money had been lost.
   b. This character had died in India.
   c. This character had hollow eyes.
   d. This character took care of a sick man.
   e. This character could not speak English.

PART F   Exaggeration

1. Here's an example of exaggeration: *The rain lasted forever.*
   a. How long does the statement say the rain lasted?
   b. Write an accurate statement that tells how long the rain lasted.
2. Here's another example: *Tatsu had a mountain of food on his plate.*
   a. How much food does the statement say that Tatsu had?
   b. Write an accurate statement that tells how much food Tatsu had.

PART G   Vocabulary Items

Use the words in the box to fill in the blanks or replace the underlined words.

rude and bold	rich and elegant
awed	smarted
delicious	vague
down-trodden	obliged
showed	deprived of
subscribe to	jostled

1. Their hands <u>stung</u> from clapping so hard.
2. He was being punished, so he was _____ his bicycle for a week.
3. The cows pushed and <u>jolted</u> her as they crowded through the gate.
4. The little boy gave them a <u>impudent</u> look and then stuck out his tongue.
5. The man threw away the <u>tattered and worn</u> coat.
6. In the center of the room was a <u>luxurious</u> silk rug.
7. The cakes in the bakery looked <u>luscious</u>.
8. He <u>vented</u> his anger on the punching bag.

PART H   Writing Assignment

Write a short story that explains why the Indian Gentleman hadn't found Sara before.

Make your story at least five sentences long.

SKILLBOOK

Testing and Management

The *Reading Mastery* series offers a complete testing program, as well as an effective management system. The testing program includes placement tests, in-program tests, and mastery tests. The placement tests determine the level in which students should be placed; the in-program and mastery tests measure student progress within each level. The management system includes specific guidelines for grouping the students, for scheduling the reading period, and for motivating the students.

Placement Tests

The students should generally be placed in the level of *Reading Mastery* that corresponds with their grade level. To ensure accurate placement, each level of the series includes a placement test. These tests should be administered at the beginning of the school year.

The placement test results will provide the teacher with

- information about the students' decoding and comprehension skills
- a means of identifying which students should be placed in another level of the *Reading Mastery* series
- guidelines for grouping the students

Copies of the placement test and accompanying instructions appear on pages 53-64 of this guide, as well as in the Teacher's Guides. These copies may be reproduced for classroom use.

In-Program Tests

The *Reading Mastery* series is designed so that the students are constantly tested as they progress through each level of the series. Each student's decoding skills are periodically measured through rate-and-accuracy checkouts. For these checkouts, the student reads a passage aloud as the teacher records the student's decoding errors. Comprehension, reference, and study skills are measured through the daily independent work. Because the independent work is directly related to the other program material, it serves as a continuous test of each student's skill mastery. The teacher checks the independent work every day and uses a chart to keep track of each student's performance.

The rate-and-accuracy checkouts and the independent work can also be used to identify students who need remedial help. The *Teacher's Guides* contains specific remedial procedures for students who do not perform well on these tasks. These procedures include a review of program material and additional practice with specific skills. The procedures can be used with individual students or with an entire group.

Mastery Tests

The mastery tests appear in the optional *Test Books*. These criterion-referenced tests are administered after every twentieth lesson. Each test item measures student mastery of a specific skill taught in the *Reading Mastery* series. The *Test Books* also include an Individual Skills Profile Chart. The chart lists the specific skills taught in *Reading Mastery* and indicates which test items measure student mastery of those skills. When the chart is completed, it shows how well a student has mastered the skills taught in *Reading Mastery*.

Instructions for administering the mastery tests appear in the *Testing and Management Handbooks*. These handbooks also contain remedial exercises for students who do not perform well on the mastery tests. Each test has its own set of remedial exercises, and there is a specific remedial exercise for every tested skill.

Grouping the Students

Reading Mastery can be presented either to small groups of students or to the entire class. In general, levels I through IV should be presented to small groups of students, while levels V and VI should be presented to the entire class.

Small-group instruction offers several advantages. If the teacher uses small-group instruction, the students can be grouped according to their ability levels: above-average, average, below-average. This homogeneous grouping will allow the teacher to spend more time with the below-average students, who will need the most help. The teacher can use the placement test results as a guideline for grouping the students.

Small-group instruction also allows the teacher to monitor individual performance more closely. In small groups, individual students will have more opportunities to read aloud and to answer the teacher's questions. The students will also get a better view of any material the teacher presents. This is particularly important in *Reading Mastery I* and *II*, where the teacher often points to words and letters in the *Presentation Book*.

Small-group instruction is simple with *Reading Mastery*, because the teacher can teach one group of students while the rest of the students are doing their independent work. Ideally, for *Reading Mastery I* and *II*, the class should be divided into three groups: above-average, average, and below-average. The below-average group should be the smallest. For *Reading Mastery III* and *IV*, the class can be divided into just two groups: one for the below-average students and another for the rest of the class. *Reading Mastery V* and *VI* are usually presented to the entire class, but they can also be presented to small groups.

Scheduling the Reading Period

Generally, one lesson of *Reading Mastery* should be presented on each day of the school year. Every lesson is divided into three parts: group instruction, independent work, and workcheck. The group instruction usually requires thirty minutes; the independent work, between twenty and thirty minutes; the workcheck, ten minutes. The students should generally complete the independent work immediately after finishing the group instruction. However, they can also complete the independent work later in the day, or even as homework.

The following chart shows one possible schedule for a *Reading Mastery* class with two groups of students.

	Group A	Group B
8:45-9:15	group instruction	
9:15-9:45	independent work	group instruction
9:45-10:15	workcheck	independent work
10:15-10:25		workcheck

Motivating the Students

Reading Mastery is designed so that every student can succeed. Every lesson is divided into a series of tasks or exercises. The students are able to succeed on each and every task, and their success is consistently rewarded. As soon as the students learn a new skill in one task, they apply that skill in another task, and review it in still another. This constant application and review provides a consistent reward for learning. Students are motivated to learn each new skill, because they know that they will soon be using that skill.

The programs also provide additional incentives for learning. In *Reading Mastery I* and *II*, the students can earn stars for reading well. In selected lessons, the teacher calls on individual students to read a story aloud. The students earn stars if they are able to read within a specific error limit. The teacher keeps a permanent record of these stars.

In *Reading Mastery III, IV, V,* and *VI*, the students can earn points for good performance. The students earn points for reading the word lists and the stories, and for their independent work. They can also earn bonus points for doing particularly well. The students record their points in the boxes that appear at the beginning of each *Workbook* lesson. The teacher totals the points and writes the totals on the Group Summary Chart. The chart can then be used as an objective basis for assigning grades. When grades are based on the daily point system, the students are motivated to earn as many points as they can. Management problems are reduced, and learning takes top priority.

Teaching Techniques

Arranging the Classroom

The classroom should be arranged differently for different levels of the program.

In *Reading Mastery I* and *II*, the teacher will usually be presenting the program to small groups of students. The group that is being taught should be seated in a small semicircle in front of the teacher. The students should sit on chairs, not at desks, and the teacher should be within touching distance of every student. Every student in the group must be able to see the words that the teacher presents from the *Presentation Book*. The problem students in the group should be seated directly in front of the teacher, where the teacher will be able to monitor them closely.

Reading Mastery III and *IV* are usually presented to somewhat larger groups of students. The group that is being taught should face the teacher. The students may sit at their desks, or simply on chairs. The group can be arranged in any form, so long as all the students are facing the teacher. The problem students should be seated directly in front of the teacher.

Reading Mastery V and *VI* are usually presented to the entire class. The class should be facing the teacher, and the students should be seated at their desks. The problem students should be seated directly in front of the teacher.

Using the Presentation Book

The *Presentation Books* contain complete scripts for presenting every lesson in *Reading Mastery*. The scripts are carefully written so that all instruction is clear and unambiguous. The program will be most effective if the scripts are followed closely.

The *Presentation Books* use several typefaces. The following typefaces are used in *Reading Mastery I* and *II*.

- This red type indicates what the teacher says.
- This black type indicates what the teacher does.
- *This italic type indicates the students' answers.*

The following typefaces are used in *Reading Mastery III, IV, V,* and *VI*.

- This type indicates what the teacher says.
- *This italic type indicates what the teacher does.*
- **This bold type indicates the students' answers to questions that require precise responses.**
- This light type indicates the basic idea of the students' answers to questions that permit varied responses.

Pacing the Lesson

The daily lessons should be presented at a lively pace. Fast pacing offers several advantages.

- Fast pacing generates student interest. Students are likely to pay attention if the lesson is presented at a lively pace.
- Fast pacing encourages student achievement. With fast pacing, a teacher can cover more material and the students can receive more practice.
- Fast pacing keeps the students thinking. If a lesson is presented slowly, the students' minds may wander. With fast pacing, the students are constantly thinking, and they are unlikely to get distracted.
- Fast pacing reduces management problems. With fast pacing, the students are involved in their work and unlikely to misbehave.

To set a fast pace, the teacher should move quickly, but should not rush the students into making mistakes. Experience will determine the pace that is appropriate for each group. The teacher should read over the material before presenting it. Fast pacing is easier if the teacher does not have to refer to the *Presentation Book* for every word.

Using Signals

For many of the tasks in *Reading Mastery*, the students must answer aloud and in unison. When the group responds in unison

- every student must initiate a response
- every student is able to practice the task
- the teacher can monitor every student
- the teacher can hear any incorrect answers and correct them immediately

In order for the students to answer simultaneously, the teacher must use a signal. By using a signal, the teacher eliminates the problem of one student leading the rest of the group.

There are two basic types of signals: visual and auditory. The visual signals are used when the students are looking at the teacher or at the *Presentation Book*. The teacher signals the students by making some type of hand motion: by quickly dropping a hand, by touching a word, or by slashing under a word. Auditory signals are used in all levels. The students answer on signal as they read word lists, stories, and skill exercises. Auditory signals are used for these tasks because the students are looking at what they are reading, and not at the teacher. The teacher can either use a clap, a finger snap, or a tap on a desk as an auditory signal.

The teacher should use the following procedure for both visual and auditory signals.

1. Ask the specified question.
2. Pause for about one second.
3. Give the auditory or visual signal.
4. Listen to the group response and correct any errors.
5. Move quickly to the next question.

The one-second pause is very important. It clearly separates the question from the signal and ensures that every student sees or hears the signal. The pause should always last for about one second. When the pause is of a consistent length, the group is able to answer more effectively.

Praising the Students

The students will work harder if they receive praise for their work. Each lesson provides many opportunities for praise. The teacher can praise the students when they learn a new sound, when they read lists of words, or when they read a story without making any errors. The teacher can also praise students when they behave well and when they work particularly hard.

Praise should be simple and positive. The teacher can say things such as, "Great. You read the entire list without making any mistakes." or "Good talking. I could hear everybody." The students are especially reinforced when the teacher repeats a correct answer; for example, "Yes, that word is **am**."

Praise should be an integral part of the teacher's presentation, but it should not be overdone. Every statement of praise should clearly result from a specific student action. If praise is indiscriminate and undeserved, it will lose all meaning for the students. Generally, students in the lower levels of the program will require more praise than students in the upper levels.

Correcting Mistakes

The *Reading Mastery* programs include correction procedures for many of the mistakes that the students are likely to make. These mistakes fall into two categories: general and specific. The general mistakes include not paying attention and not answering on signal. The specific mistakes include misidentifying words and giving the wrong answers to questions.

General Mistakes

The general mistakes are most likely to occur when students are beginning the program. It is very important to correct these mistakes as soon as they occur, so that students do not fall into bad habits.

In *Reading Mastery I* and *II*, the students must always pay attention when the teacher is pointing to letters or words in the *Presentation Book*. If a student is not paying attention, the teacher should use the following procedure.

1. Look at the student.
2. Say, "Watch my finger. Let's try it again."
3. Repeat the question as soon as the student is paying attention.
4. Return to the beginning of the task.

Variations of this procedure can be used whenever a student is not paying attention. The teacher should always look at the student, tell the student to pay attention, repeat the question, and then return to the beginning of the task.

If a student is paying attention, but does not answer a question, the teacher should use the following procedure.

1. Look at the student.
2. Say, "I have to hear everybody."
3. Repeat the question.
4. Return to the beginning of the task.

Every student must answer exactly on signal. A student who does not answer on signal may begin to depend on the other students for the correct answers. The correction procedure shows the students that the teacher expects everyone to answer on signal.

If a student answers early or late, the teacher should use the following procedure.

1. Look at the student.
2. Say, "You're early," or "You're late."
3. Repeat the question until all the students answer on signal.
4. Return to the beginning of the task.

By requiring a simultaneous response, the teacher eliminates the problem of one student leading and the others following. When the students answer simultaneously, they have to think for themselves, and they will pay closer attention to the teacher.

In all of these procedures, the teacher must first correct the mistake and then return to the beginning of the task. By repeating the task, the teacher demonstrates to the students that mistakes will not be ignored. The students must work on a task from beginning to end until they get it right. If general mistakes are properly corrected in the early lessons of a program, the students will make far fewer mistakes in the later lessons.

Specific Mistakes

When students misidentify a word or give a wrong answer, they are making a specific mistake. Many of the tasks in the *Presentation Books* contain correction procedures for specific mistakes. There are two basic types of correction procedures for specific mistakes. The first type is the *model-lead-test-retest* procedure. The second type is the *process-test-retest* procedure.

Here is an example of the *model-lead-test-retest* procedure.

To correct
If the children do not say *aaa:*
1. **aaa.**
2. Touch the first ball of the arrow. **Say it with me. Get ready.** Move quickly to the second ball of the arrow. Hold for two seconds. Say **aaa** with the children. *aaa.*
3. Touch the first ball of the arrow. **Your turn. Get ready.** Move quickly to the second ball of the arrow. Hold for two seconds. *aaa.*

In step 1, the teacher *models* the correct answer. In step 2, the teacher *leads* the students by saying the correct answer with them. (Sometimes, the *lead* step is not used.) In step 3, the teacher *tests* the students by having them say the correct answer by themselves. At a later point in the lesson, the teacher *retests* the students by presenting the task again.

Here is an example of the *process-test-retest* procedure.

To correct
1. **Everybody, sound out the word.** Touch each sound as the children sound out the word.
2. **What word?** (Signal.)

In step 1, the students use a particular *process* to correct their mistakes. In this case, the process is to sound out the word. In step 2, the teacher *tests* the students by asking, "What word"? At a later point in the lesson, the teacher *retests* by presenting the task again.

The specific correction procedures typically appear when a new skill is introduced, because that is when the students are most likely to make mistakes. If the students are properly corrected at this time, they are unlikely to make mistakes when the skill appears in subsequent tasks. Nevertheless, the teacher should memorize the correction procedure for a particular skill so that it can be administered at any time.

Teaching to Mastery

Every skill in *Reading Mastery* should be taught to mastery. When a skill is taught to mastery, every student in the group is able to perform the skill independently, without making any mistakes.

Teaching to mastery is of critical importance, because the students are constantly applying each new skill. When a skill is taught to mastery, the students are able to apply the skill and are prepared to learn related skills. By teaching every skill to mastery, the teacher ensures that each student is able to succeed throughout the program.

Practice Scripts

This section contains representative teacher presentation scripts from each level of the *Reading Mastery* series. If you will be teaching *Reading Mastery*, you should practice the appropriate scripts before presenting the program to your students. You can practice the scripts on your own, with another teacher, or at a training session conducted by an experienced trainer.

To practice a script, first read the script carefully and become familiar with it. Then present the script aloud several times, with only brief glances at the actual text. During these presentations, you should execute the proper signals and develop a rapid pace. Finally, present the script to another person, who will play the role of the student. This "student" can then answer on signal and can also make intentional errors that you have to correct.

You should practice the scripts that are relevant to the program level you will be teaching. The following chart shows the practice scripts that are relevant to each level.

Level	Practice Scripts
I	1, 2, 3, 4, 5, 9
II	3, 4, 5, 9, 10
III	6, 7, 8, 10
IV	6, 7, 8, 10
V	6, 7, 8, 10
VI	6, 7, 8, 10

If time permits, you should practice the remaining scripts. This additional practice will give you a valuable perspective on the entire series.

Practice Script 1

The following script appears in lesson 4 of *Reading Mastery I*. The script introduces the sound **mmm**.

TASK 5   Introducing the new sound mmm as in mat

a. Touch the first ball of the arrow. Here's a new sound. My turn to say it. When I move under the sound, I'll say it. I'll keep on saying it as long as I touch under it. Get ready. Move quickly to the second ball of the arrow. Hold for two seconds. **mmm**.

b. Touch the first ball of the arrow. My turn again. Get ready. Move quickly to the second ball of the arrow. Hold for two seconds. **mmm**.

c. Touch the first ball of the arrow. My turn again. Get ready. Move quickly to the second ball of the arrow. Hold for two seconds. **mmm**.

d. Touch the first ball of the arrow. Your turn. When I move under the sound, you say it. Keep on saying it as long as I touch under it. Get ready. Move quickly to the second ball of the arrow. Hold for two seconds. *mmm*. Yes, **mmm**.

To correct

If the children do not say *mmm:*

1. *mmm*.
2. Touch the first ball of the arrow. Say it with me. Get ready. Move quickly to the second ball of the arrow. Hold for two seconds. Say *mmm* with the children. *mmm*.
3. Touch the first ball of the arrow. Your turn. Get ready. Move quickly to the second ball of the arrow. Hold for two seconds. *mmm*.

---

e. Touch the first ball of the arrow. Again. Get ready. Move quickly to the second ball of the arrow. Hold for two seconds. *mmm*. Yes, **mmm**.

f. Repeat *e* until firm.

g. Call on different children to do *d*.

h. Good saying **mmm**.

Description

In steps a–c, you model the correct way to say the sound. In step d, you test the students by having them say the sound. Step d also includes a correction procedure. In steps e and f, you continue to test the students until all of them have mastered the sound. Finally, in step g, individual students take turns saying the sound.

Teaching Techniques

You should hold the *Presentation Book* so that all the students can see the sound. Hold the book with one hand and point with the other hand. Use the following procedures to present the sound.

1. Touch the large ball of the arrow and say, "Your turn. Get ready."
2. Pause for one second.
3. Quickly move your finger to the second ball of the arrow. This movement acts as a signal for the students to say the sound.
4. Touch the second ball for two seconds. Because **mmm** is a continuous sound, the students say the sound for as long as you touch the second ball.

When presenting this task, make sure that you do not block the students' view of the letter. Always touch the balls, not the letter. Also, make sure that your signal timing is consistent. Always pause for one second before moving to the second ball, and always point to the second ball for two seconds.

Step f requires you to repeat step e until all students are "firm." Students are "firm" when every one of them has mastered the sound. Every student must be able to say the sound for as long as you touch it.

In step g, you test individual students. You do not have to give an individual test to every student on every task. However, during the course of a lesson, every student should receive at least two or three individual tests. Try to give most individual tests to the slower students in the group, so that you can be sure that they have mastered each task.

Correcting Mistakes

To correct mistakes, use the specified correction procedure.

1. *Model* the correct answer by saying the sound.
2. *Lead* the students by saying the sound with them.
3. *Test* the students by having them say the sound by themselves.

In order to provide a *retest*, present the sound again at a later point in the lesson.

Practice Script 2

The following script appears in lesson 27 of *Reading Mastery I*. The script introduces the sound **d**.

TASK 2   Introducing the new sound d as in dad

---

a. Touch the ball of the arrow for **d**. We always have to say this sound fast. The little arrow under the sound tells me that I can't stop under this sound. My turn to say it fast. Slash to the end of the arrow as you say d. Return to the ball. My turn to say it fast again. Slash to the end of the arrow as you say d.

b. Touch the ball of the arrow. Your turn. Say it fast. Slash to the end of the arrow. *d.* Yes, **d.**

c. Repeat *b* until firm.

d. Call on different children to do *b*.

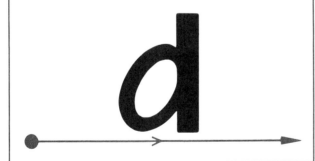

Description

This script is similar to practice script 1, except that the presentation has been streamlined and the correction procedure no longer appears. (Printed correction procedures are included only in the first few appearances of a task, but they can still be used to correct student errors on subsequent appearances of the task, or on similar tasks.)

In step a, you model the correct way to say the sound. In step b, you test the students by having them say the sound. In step c, you continue to test the students until all of them have mastered the sound. Finally, in step d, individual students take turns saying the sound.

Teaching Techniques

Because **d** is a stop sound, you signal differently than for **mmm**.

1. Touch the large ball and say, "Your turn. Say it fast."
2. Pause for one second.
3. Slash your finger under the sound. This slash acts as a signal. When your finger passes under the sound, the students "say it fast."

Corrections

To correct mistakes, use the *model-lead-test-retest* procedure.

1. *Model* the correct answer by saying the sound.
2. *Lead* the students by saying the sound with them.
3. *Test* the students by having them say the sound by themselves.
4. *Retest* the students by presenting the sound again at a later point in the lesson.

Practice Script 3

The following script appears in lesson 5 of *Reading Mastery II*. The script reviews sounds that the students have learned: **u** as in *under*, **ch** as in *chat*, **d** as in *mad*, **m** as in *ram*.

TASK 1 Sounds firm-up

a. Point to the sounds.
Get ready to tell me these sounds.
b. When I touch it, you say it.
Keep on saying it as long as I touch it.
c. Point to each sound. Get ready.
Touch the sound. *The children say the sound.*
Lift your finger.

To correct

1. Immediately say the correct sound as you continue to touch it. Lift your finger.
2. **Say it with me.** Touch the sound and say it with children. Lift your finger.
3. **Again.** Repeat until firm.
4. **All by yourselves. Get ready.** Touch the sound. *The children say the sound.*

---

d. Repeat problem sounds until the children can correctly identify all sounds in order.

Individual test

Call on several children to identify one or more sounds.

Description

In steps a-c, you test the students by having them say each sound. Step c also includes a correction procedure. In step d, you retest the students until you are sure that they have mastered each sound. Finally, you administer individual tests.

Teaching Techniques

Your presentation is different than in the preceding scripts, because there are no arrows under the sounds.

1. Point just below a sound, with your finger about an inch from the page.
2. Say, "Get ready."
3. Pause for one second.
4. Touch under the sound. Your touch acts as a signal. Always touch under the letter, so that all the students can see the letter.

The students say the sound for as long as you touch under it. Touch continuous sounds, such as **u** and **m**, for two seconds; touch stop sounds, such as **ch** and **d**, for just an instant.

Corrections

To correct mistakes, use the specified correction procedure.

1. *Model* the correct answer by saying the sound.
2. *Lead* the students by saying the sound with them. (You may need to repeat this step several times.)
3. *Test* the students by having them say the sound by themselves.
4. *Retest* the students by proceeding to step d.

Practice Script 4

The following script appears in lesson 46 of *Reading Mastery I*. The script introduces the word **meat**.

TASK 9 Children sound out the word and say it fast

a. Touch the first ball of the arrow for **mēat**. **Sound it out. Get ready.** Move quickly under each sound. *Mmmēēēt.*

b. Return to the first ball. **Again, sound it out. Get ready.** Move quickly under each sound. *Mmmēēēt.*

c. Repeat *b* until firm.

d. Return to the first ball. **Say it fast.** Slash. *Meat.* **Yes, what word?** *Meat.* **A hamburger is made of** (pause) **meat.**

Description

In steps a-c, the students sound out the word by saying each sound in sequence. Then, in step d, the students read the word normally by "saying it fast."

Teaching Techniques

To present the word, follow this procedure.

1. Touch the large ball and say, "Sound it out. Get ready."
2. Pause for one second.
3. Quickly move your finger to the second ball of the arrow. Hold your finger on the second ball for about one second, as the students say **mmm**.
4. Move your finger to the third ball and hold it there for about second, as the students say **eee** .
5. Move your finger to the fourth ball and hold it there for just an instant, as the students say **t**.

Note that the small **a** does not have a ball under it. The students do not say any small silent letters; you simply move your finger past them.

After the students are proficient at sounding out the word, they "say it fast." Use the following procedure.

1. Touch the large ball of the arrow and say, "Say it fast."
2. Pause for one second.
3. Quickly slash under the word as the students "say it fast."

Corrections

Some students may have trouble "saying it fast." To correct mistakes, use a *model-test-retest* procedure.

1. *Model* the correct answer by sounding out the word and saying it fast.
2. *Test* the students by having them sound out the word and say it fast.
3. *Retest* the students by presenting the task again at later point in the lesson.

Practice Script 5

The following script appears in lesson 11 of *Reading Mastery II*.

TASK 10 Read the fast way

a. Read these words the fast way.
b. Touch the ball for **another.**
(Pause two seconds.) Get ready. (Signal.)
Another. Yes, **another.**

To correct
Have the children sound out and tell what word.

c. Repeat *b* for **whȳ, when,** and **funny.**

another

whȳ

when

funny

Description

This task reviews words that the students have already learned. The students read all the words "the fast way," without first sounding them out.

Teaching Techniques

To present the words, follow this procedure.

1. Touch the ball of the arrow.
2. Pause for two seconds. This pause gives the students time to examine the word.
3. Say, "Get ready."
4. Pause for one second.
5. Quickly slash under the word with your finger, as the students read the word.
6. Reinforce the students by repeating the word out loud.

Corrections

Correct mistakes by using a *process- test-retest* procedure.

1. Tell the students to use the sounding-out *process,* and direct them as they sound out the word.
2. *Test* the students by asking them, "What word"?
3. *Retest* the students by returning to the top of the column and presenting all of the words in order.

Practice Script 6

Beginning in *Reading Mastery III*, the word lists are printed in the students' books. The *Presentation Books* contain presentation scripts for the word lists, as well as reproductions of the student material.

The following script appears in lesson 10 of *Reading Mastery IV*.

2
gloves
escape
peanuts
sunlight
hallelujah

EXERCISE 2   Word practice

1. Everybody, touch under the first word in column 2. *Pause.* What word? *Signal.* **Gloves.**
2. Next word. *Pause.* What word? *Signal.* **Escape.**

To correct word-identification errors (escape, for example):
   a. That word is **escape.**
   What word? *Signal.* **Escape.**
   b. Spell **escape.** *Signal.* **E-s-c-a-p-e.**
   c. What word did you spell? *Signal.* **Escape.**
   d. *Repeat the column, starting with the first word.*

---

3. *Repeat step 2 for each remaining word in column 2.*
4. *Repeat the words in column 2 until firm.*

Description

In steps 1-3, you test the students by having them read each word aloud.

In step 4, you continue to test the students until you are sure that they have mastered all of the words.

Teaching Techniques

To present the word lists, follow this procedure.

1. Direct the students to look at a particular word.
2. Pause for two seconds. This pause gives the students time to examine the word.
3. Say, "What word?"
4. Pause for one second.
5. Give an auditory signal. You must give an auditory signal, such as a clap, a tap, or a finger snap, because the students are looking at their books, and not at you.
6. Listen carefully as the students say the word.

Corrections

To correct mistakes, use the specified correction procedure.

1. *Model* the correct answer by saying the word.
2. *Test* the students by having them say the word.
3. Have the students spell the word.
4. *Test* the students again by having them say the word.
5. *Retest* the students by repeating the entire column.

Practice Script 7

Beginning in *Reading Mastery III*, the teacher presents vocabulary exercises after the students have finished reading the word lists. The following vocabulary script appears in lesson 52 of *Reading Mastery III*.

Description

In task A, you direct the students as they read the list of vocabulary words. In tasks B through E, you teach the meaning of each word, using a variety of methods.

In step 1 of task B, you present a word and its meaning. Then, in step 2, you test the students by giving the meaning. The students must then say the word in unison.

In tasks C and D, you use a more complicated method. In step 1, you first present a word and its meaning. Then you use the word in context. In steps 2 and 3, you test the students by having them use the word in context.

In task E, you use still another method. You simply call on a student to give a word's meaning. Because the students' answers may vary, the correct answer is preceded by the word *Idea*. Accept any answers that express the correct idea.

Although many different methods are used to present vocabulary words, they all follow the same basic pattern. First you present a vocabulary word and its meaning, or have a student give the meaning. Then you test the students by having them say the vocabulary word in response to its meaning, or by having them use the vocabulary word in sentence context. When they are tested, the students must answer in unison.

Teaching Techniques

When presenting the word list in task A, use the same teaching techniques discussed in practice script 6. For tasks B through E, however, your techniques will be somewhat different. To begin with, you should tell the students to look at you, because they will have finished reading the word lists. Your signal will be slightly different when the students are looking at you.

6

Vocabulary words

1. gate
2. flight
3. thaw
4. breeze

EXERCISE 3   Vocabulary words

Task A

1. Everybody, touch column 6. *Check.*
   First you're going to read the words in column 6. Then we'll talk about what they mean.
2. Touch under the first word. *Pause.*
   What word? *Signal.* **Gate.**
3. Next word. *Pause.*
   What word? *Signal.* **Flight.**
4. *Repeat step 3 for each remaining word in column 6.*
5. *Repeat the words in column 6 until firm.*

Task B

1. Now let's talk about what those words mean. Word 1 is **gate.** The place where a jet parks at an airport is called a gate.
2. Everybody, what's the name for the place where a jet parks at an airport? *Signal.* **A gate.**

Task C

1. Word 2 is **flight.** Another name for a **plane trip** is a **flight.** Here's another way of saying **The plane trip to Chicago: the flight to Chicago.**
2. Your turn. What's another way of saying **the plane trip to Chicago?** *Signal.* The flight to Chicago. *Repeat step 2 until firm.*
3. What's another way of saying **the plane trip to New York City?** *Signal.* The flight to New York City.

Task D

1. Word 3 is **thaw.** When a frozen thing **thaws,** the water in it melts. Here's another way of saying **The ice cube is melting: The ice cube is thawing.**
2. Your turn. What's another way of saying **The ice cream is melting?** *Signal.*
   The ice cream is thawing.
   Repeat step 2 until firm.
3. What's another way of saying **The snow is melting?** *Signal.*
   The snow is thawing.

Task E

1. Word 4 is **breeze.**
   Call on a student. What's a **breeze?**
   Idea: A soft wind.

1. Hold out one hand, as if you were stopping traffic.
2. Present the question.
3. Pause for one second.
4. Quickly drop your hand. Your hand-drop acts as a signal. If you want, you can also snap your fingers as you drop your hand.
5. Listen carefully to the students' answers and correct any mistakes.

Corrections

Some students may have trouble using the vocabulary words in context. For example, in step 2 of task D, they may say, "The ice cream is melting." instead of, "The ice cream is thawing." Use a *model-test-retest* procedure to correct mistakes.

1. *Model* the correct answer by saying it.
2. *Test* the students by having them repeat the correct answer.
3. *Test* the students again by repeating the question.
4. *Retest* the students by repeating the question at a later point in the lesson.

Practice Script 8

In certain lessons, the teacher directs the students as they read skill exercises that appear in their *Skillbooks* or *Workbooks*. The following script appears in lesson 50 of *Reading Mastery VI*.

Description

The students take turns reading the exercise aloud. At each circled letter, the teacher presents the questions specified in the *Presentation Book*. These questions are always presented to individual students.

Teaching Techniques

Because all of the questions are presented to individual students, no signals are used. Call on a different student to answer each question. Below-average students should be called on the most, so that you can be sure they have mastered the skill.

Corrections

Use a *model-test-retest* procedure to correct mistakes.

1. Present the task to another student, who will *model* the correct answer.
2. *Test* the first student by repeating the question.
3. *Retest* the first student by repeating the question at a later point in the lesson.

EXERCISE 4 Figurative language: metaphors

1. Everybody, look at part D. *Check.*
2. *Call on individual students to read. Present the tasks specified for each circled letter.*
(A) Name the figurative language that is like a simile. **Metaphor.**
• How is a metaphor different from a simile? *Idea:* Does not contain the word like.
(B) What's the answer? **Clouds, gray ceiling.**
(C) What's the answer? *Ideas:* Both cover your head; can't see through them.
(D) What's the answer? **Sara's attic room, a nest.**
(E) What's the answer? *Ideas:* Both are near the top; both are comfortable places.
• You'll write the answers to the items later.

PART D Metaphors

A metaphor is like a simile except that it doesn't contain the word *like.*(A)

1. Here's an accurate statement: *Gray clouds covered the sky.* Here's a metaphor: *The clouds were a gray ceiling.*
   a. What two things are the same in that metaphor?(B)
   b. How could they be the same?(C)
2. Here's another metaphor: *Sara's attic room was a nest in a tree.*
   a. What two things are the same in that metaphor?(D)
   b. How could they be the same?(E)
3. Here's another metaphor: *The boxer's arms were lightning bolts.*
   a. What two things are the same in that metaphor?
   b. How could they be the same?

Practice Script 9

There are two basic procedures for presenting the Group Reading. The first procedure is used in *Reading Mastery I* and lessons 1-80 of *Reading Mastery II*. The following script shows the first procedure. It appears in lesson 14 of *Reading Mastery II*.

Description

In task 12, the students read the title and the first part of the story aloud and in unison. In task 13, the students take turns reading the rest of the story aloud. You call on different students to read one sentence each. Occasionally, you direct the group to read a sentence in unison. In task 14, the students take turns reading the story again, as you present comprehension questions.

Teaching Techniques

Use the following procedure to conduct the reading.

1. Direct the students to touch under each word by saying, "First word," or "Next word."
2. Pause for two seconds. This pause gives the students time to examine the word.
3. Say, "Get ready."
4. Pause for one second.
5. Clap your hands, as the students read the word in unison.

The comprehension questions are cued by little numbers in your copy of the story. When the students read up to a number, you present the questions for that number. Sentences that contain numbers are always underlined. The students' version of the text does not contain any numbers or underlines.

The students should be looking at you when you present the questions, but they should continue to touch the current word in the story. For questions that require precise answers, you will need to use a hand-drop signal.

1. Hold out one hand, as if you were stopping traffic.
2. Present the question.
3. Pause for one second.
4. Quickly drop your hand. Your hand-drop acts as a signal. If you want, you can also snap your fingers as you drop your hand.
5. Listen carefully to the students' answers and correct any mistakes.

Some comprehension questions do not require precise answers. You simply present these questions to the group and accept all reasonable answers.

Corrections

The students will make two basic types of mistakes during the Group Reading: word-identification errors and comprehension errors. To correct word-identification errors, follow the procedure specified in task 14.

1. *Model* the correct answer by saying the word.
2. *Test* the student by having the student say the word.
3. *Retest* the student by having the student reread the sentence.

Comprehension errors tend to fall into two groups. For some questions, the students will give the right answer, but they will say it incorrectly. For other questions, the students will simply give the wrong answer.

When the students do not say the answer correctly, use the following procedure.

1. *Model* the correct answer by saying the answer correctly.
2. *Test* the students by having them say the answer correctly.
3. *Retest* the students by repeating the question.

The corrections for wrong answers are a little more complicated. If the question is clearly answered by a sentence in the story, use the following procedure.

1. Demonstrate a *process* for answering the question by rereading the appropriate sentence.
2. *Test* the students by repeating the question.
3. *Retest* the students by repeating the question again at a later point in the lesson.

If the question is not clearly answered by a sentence in the story, use the following procedure.

1. *Model* the correct answer by saying the correct answer.
2. *Test* the students by having them say the correct answer.
3. *Test* the students again by repeating the question.
4. *Retest* the students by repeating the question at a later point in the lesson.

TASK 12 First reading—title and three sentences

a. Everybody, open your reader to page 22.
b. Everybody, touch the title.
Check to see that the children are touching under the first word of the title.
c. I'll clap and you read each word in the title the fast way. Don't sound it out. Just tell me the word.
d. First word. Check children's responses. (Pause two seconds.) Get ready. Clap. The children read *the*.
e. Next word. Check children's responses. (Pause two seconds.) Get ready. Clap. The children read *cow*.
f. Repeat *e* for the remaining words in the title.
g. Everybody, say the title. (Signal.)
The cow boy and the cow.
Yes, **the cow boy and the cow.**
h. Everybody, get ready to read this story the fast way.
i. First word. Check children's responses. (Pause two seconds.) Get ready. Clap. *A.*
j. Next word. Check children's responses. (Pause two seconds.) Get ready. Clap. *Cow boy.*
k. Repeat *j* for the remaining words in the first three sentences. Have the children reread the first three sentences until firm.

TASK 13 Remaining sentences

a. I'm going to call on different children to read a sentence. Everybody, follow along and point to the words. If you hear a mistake, raise your hand.
b. Call on a child. Read the next sentence.
c. Call on a different child.
Read the next sentence.
d. Repeat *c* for most of the remaining sentences in the story.
e. Occasionally have the group read a sentence.

TASK 14 Second reading—sentences and questions

a. You're going to read the story again.
This time I'm going to ask questions.
b. Starting with the first word of the title.
Check children's responses. Get ready.
Clap as the children read the title.
c. Call on a child. Read the first sentence.

To correct word-identification errors
(**from**, for example)
1. That word is **from**. What word? *From.*
2. Go back to the beginning of the sentence and read the sentence again.

---

d. Call on a different child.
Read the next sentence.
e. Repeat *d* for most of the remaining sentences in the story.
f. Occasionally have the group read a sentence.
g. After each underlined sentence has been read, present each comprehension question specified below to the entire group.

[1]What's this story going to be about?
(Signal.) *The cow boy and the cow.*
What do cow boys usually ride on? (Signal.)
Horses.
[2]Why was this cow boy sad? (Signal.)
He did not have a horse.
[3]What did the cow say? (Signal.)
But I can run as fast as a horse.
[4]Do you think the cow can really jump better than a horse?
The children respond. We'll see.
[5]Is the cow boy going to give the cow a try?
(Signal.) *Yes.*
[6]Why did the other cow boys make fun of him? *The children respond.*
[7]Is this the end of the story? (Signal.)
No. Next time we'll read more about the cow boy and the cow.

---

the cow boy and the cow[1]
a cow boy was sad. hē did not havₑ a hōrsₑ.[2] the other cow boys said, "hō, hō, that funny cow boy has nō hōrsₑ."
a cow cāmₑ up to the cow boy. the cow said, "if you arₑ a cow boy, you nēēd a cow. I am a cow."

the cow boy said, "do not bē funny. cow boys do not rīdₑ on cows."
the cow said, "but I can run as fast as a hōrsₑ.[3] and I can jump better than a hōrsₑ."[4]
the cow boy said, "I will givₑ you a trȳ. but I will fēēl very funny rīdiñg on a cow." sō

the cow boy got on the cow.[5]
then the other cow boys cāmₑ up the rōad. "hō, hō," they said. "look at that funny cow boy.[6] hē is trȳiñg to rīdₑ a cow."
stop[7]

Practice Script 10

The second type of Group Reading procedure is used in lessons 81-160 of *Reading Mastery II* and in *Reading Mastery III, IV, V* and *VI*. The following script for a comprehension passage is typical. It appears in lesson 72 of *Reading Mastery V*.

EXERCISE 7   Comprehension passage

1. Everybody, turn to page 274 in your textbook. *Wait*.
2. *Call on individual students to read. Present the tasks specified for each circled letter.*

Ⓐ Where did they think the gods lived? *Idea:* On Mount Olympus; on a mountain.

Ⓑ What was the name of the chief god? **Zeus.**

Ⓒ What are some of the things that Zeus commanded? *Ideas:* The winds; the clouds; lightning; thunder.

• How wise was he? *Idea:* He knew everything.

Ⓓ What was the name of the god of light? **Apollo.**

• What else was he the god of? **Music.**

Ⓔ What was the name of the Greek god of the sea? **Poseidon.**

• What did Poseidon rule? **The sea.**

• Where did he live? **In an underwater palace.**

Ⓕ Who was the god of travelers? **Hermes.**

Ⓖ What was another name for Hermes? **Quicksilver.**

Ⓗ What did Hermes wear on his head? *Idea:* A helmet with wings.

Greek Gods

This passage tells about four Greek Gods. Today, you will start reading a story that tells about two of those gods.

The Greeks who lived three thousand years ago believed that there were many gods. They thought that some of these gods lived on a mountain named Mount Olympus. Ⓐ

Zeus was the chief god. Ⓑ Zeus commanded the winds, the clouds, lightning, and thunder. He was so wise that he saw everything and knew everything. He rewarded things that were good and punished things that were evil. He punished evil with storms or tornados or floods. Ⓒ

Apollo was the god of many things. But he was most important as the god of light and the god of music. Ⓓ

Poseidon was the god of the sea. Poseidon was a brother of Zeus. Poseidon could make earthquakes and great storms at sea. He lived in an underwater palace. Ⓔ

Hermes was the god of travelers. Ⓕ Hermes protected travelers and guided them. Hermes was the messenger of Zeus, and he was an extremely fast runner. He was incredibly fast. He is sometimes known as Quicksilver. Ⓖ Hermes wore a helmet with wings on it. He carried a staff that had wings and snakes on it. Hermes was also famous for playing jokes on people. Ⓗ

Description

Individual students take turns reading the passage aloud. At each circled letter, you present the comprehension questions.

For questions that require precise answers, the answers are printed in bold type. For questions that do not require precise answers, the answers are preceded by the word *Idea* and printed in light type.

Teaching Techniques

The students should look at you when you present the comprehension questions. In this practice script, all of the questions are presented to individual students, and no signal is required. However, in some Group Reading scripts, certain questions are presented to the entire group. Use a hand-drop signal for these questions. (The hand-drop signal is discussed in practice script 7.)

Corrections

The students will make two basic types of mistakes during the Group Reading: word-identification errors and comprehension errors. To correct word-identification errors, use the following procedure.

1. *Model* the correct answer by saying the word.
2. *Test* the student by having the student say the word.
3. *Retest* the student by having the student reread the sentence.

To correct comprehension errors, use the following procedure.

1. Call on another student to *model* the correct answer.
2. *Test* the first student by repeating the question.
3. *Retest* the first student by repeating the question at a later point in the lesson.

Fast Cycle

The *Fast Cycle* program is intended for above-average students in the first grade. The program is an accelerated version of *Reading Mastery I* and *II*. It consists of 170 lessons, and it can be completed in one year. After students complete *Fast Cycle*, they should be placed in *Reading Mastery III*.

Fast Cycle includes many tasks from *Reading Mastery I* and *II*, but it presents the tasks on an accelerated schedule. For example, in *Reading Mastery I*, a new letter is generally introduced in every fourth lesson; in *Fast Cycle*, a new letter is generally introduced in every second lesson. The faster rate is appropriate for above-average students.

The placement test for *Reading Mastery I* can be used to determine if students should be placed in *Fast Cycle*. The test appears on pages 53-55 of this guide.

Materials

For the teacher:

- *Presentation Books* (4)
- *Teacher's Guide*
- *Spelling Book*
- *Teacher's Take-Home Book*
- *Behavioral Objectives*
- *Skills Profile Folder*

For the students:

- *Storybooks* (2)
- *Take-Home Books* (4)

Scope and Sequence Chart

The following scope and sequence chart provides an overview of the skills taught in the *Reading Mastery* series. The skills are divided into four principal areas: decoding skills, comprehension skills, literary skills, and study skills.

Decoding Skills

Reading Mastery uses a widely acclaimed phonics method that features step-by-step instruction for all decoding skills.

Decoding Readiness: Students learn blending, sequencing, and matching skills that prepare them for decoding.

Sounds and Letters: Students learn letter sounds in a carefully programmed sequence. New letters are introduced every few lessons, and then systematically reviewed.

Words: Students learn how to sound out and read regularly spelled words and how to read irregularly spelled words.

Sentences and Stories: Students learn how to read sentences, and then entire stories. Individual checkouts monitor reading rate and accuracy.

Comprehension Skills

Reading Mastery provides thorough instruction in reading comprehension. Oral questions, written questions, and skill exercises develop comprehension in four important areas.

Comprehension Readiness: Students learn how to follow directions and how to answer questions about pictures.

Vocabulary: Students learn how to identify word meanings and how to interpret definitions.

Literal Comprehension: Students learn how to understand the explicit meaning of a text.

Interpretive Comprehension: Students learn how to interpret the implicit meaning of a text.

Reasoning: Students learn how to analyze the underlying logic of a text.

Literary Skills

Reading Mastery stresses literary appreciation and interpretation. Students read a wide range of literature and carefully analyze content and style.

Characters and Settings: Students learn how to interpret complex characters and settings.

Literary Devices: Students learn how to interpret figurative language and other elements of literary style.

Types of Literature: Students learn about various types of literature and read examples of each type.

Study Skills

Reading Mastery teaches the writing and reference skills that are necessary for effective studying.

Writing: Students gradually develop writing skills, first by copying words and stories, then by writing answers to questions, and finally by writing whole paragraphs, stories, and poems.

Reference Materials: Students learn how to interpret a wide variety of reference materials, such as maps, diagrams, time lines, and graphs.

Decoding Skills

	Fast Cycle	I	II	III	IV	V	VI
Decoding Readiness							
pronouncing individual sounds	X	X					
sequencing from left to right	X	X					
blending sounds orally	X	X					
identifying rhyming sounds	X	X					
Sounds and Letters							
reading short vowels	X	X	X				
reading long vowels	X	X	X				
reading voiced consonants	X	X	X				
reading unvoiced consonants	X	X	X				
reading sound combinations	X	X	X	X			
identifying vowel names	X		X				
identifying consonant names	X		X				
identifying alphabetical order	X		X				
Words							
reading regularly spelled words	X	X	X	X	X	X	X
reading irregularly spelled words	X	X	X	X	X	X	X
recognizing rhyming words	X	X					
recognizing inflected endings	X	X					
recognizing compound words	X		X				
reading words lists for accuracy	X		X	X	X		
spelling difficult words	X		X	X	X		
Sentences and Stories							
reading aloud	X	X	X	X	X	X	X
reading silently	X	X	X	X	X	X	X
reading aloud for rate and accuracy	X	X	X	X	X	X	
identifying punctuation marks	X	X					

Comprehension Skills

	Fast Cycle	I	II	III	IV	V	VI
Comprehension Readiness							
following oral directions	x	x	x	x	x	x	x
answering questions about pictures	x	x	x	x	x	x	
associating pictures with words	x	x					
drawing pictures based on a story	x	x					
repeating sentences	x	x					
Vocabulary							
identifying the meanings of common words	x	x	x	x	x	x	x
writing the names of pictured objects	x	x	x				
comprehending vocabulary definitions				x	x	x	x
using vocabulary words in context				x	x	x	x
identifying homonyms and homographs				x			
comprehending contractions				x			
using context to predict word meaning						x	x
Literal Comprehension							
answering literal questions about a text	x	x	x	x	x	x	x
identifying literal cause and effect	x	x	x	x	x	x	x
recalling details and events	x	x	x	x	x	x	x
following written directions	x	x	x	x	x	x	x
memorizing facts and rules	x		x	x	x		
sequencing narrative events				x	x	x	x
Interpretive Comprehension							
predicting narrative outcomes	x	x	x	x	x	x	x
relating titles to story content	x	x	x	x	x	x	
inferring causes and effects	x		x	x	x	x	x
inferring story details and events	x		x	x	x	x	x
making comparisons				x	x	x	x
inferring details relevant to a main idea					x	x	x
inferring the main idea						x	x
outlining						x	x
inferring story morals						x	
Reasoning							
using rules to classify objects	x		x	x	x		
completing written deductions	x		x	x			
drawing conclusions				x	x	x	x
using rules to predict outcomes				x	x		
evaluating problems and solutions					x	x	x
identifying relevant evidence							x
identifying contradictions							x
identifying inferential questions							x
identifying logical fallacies							x

Literary Skills

	Fast Cycle	I	II	III	IV	V	VI
Character and Settings							
interpreting a character's feelings	X	X	X	X	X	X	X
pretending to be a character	X	X	X	X	X	X	X
interpreting a character's motives	X		X	X	X	X	X
inferring a character's point of view	X	X	X	X	X	X	X
predicting a character's actions					X	X	X
identifying features of a setting					X	X	X
identifying a character's traits						X	X
Literary Devices							
interpreting figurative language							X
interpreting extended dialogues							X
interpreting substitute words							X
interpreting shortened sentences							X
interpreting combined sentences							X
interpreting literary irony							X
Types of Literature							
reading realistic fiction	X	X	X	X	X	X	X
reading fantasy	X	X	X	X	X	X	X
reading factual articles	X		X	X	X	X	X
distinguishing between realism and fantasy				X			
distinguishing between fact and fiction						X	
reading biographies						X	X
reading poetry						X	X
reading drama							X

Study Skills

	Fast Cycle	I	II	III	IV	V	VI
Writing							
copying letters	X	X	X				
copying words	X	X					
copying sentences	X	X	X				
writing answers to questions	X		X	X	X	X	X
organizing information					X	X	
completing writing assignments					X	X	X
Reference Materials							
interpreting maps				X	X	X	X
interpreting standard measurements				X	X		
interpreting diagrams				X	X		
interpreting time lines				X	X	X	
filling out forms				X			X
using reference sources					X	X	X
interpreting glossaries						X	
interpreting indexes						X	
interpreting graphs							X

Placement Tests

The placement tests can be used to determine the level of *Reading Mastery* in which your students should be placed. There is a separate test for each level.

Ideally, placement testing should be conducted at the beginning of the school year. Begin placement testing by giving your students the placement test that corresponds with their grade level. For example, students in third grade should be given the placement test for *Reading Mastery III*.

The following sections give specific instructions for each placement test.

Reading Mastery I

The placement test for *Reading Mastery I* is administered to individual students in turn. You present test items aloud and tally the student's correct answers on a score sheet. You should administer the test in a place that is somewhat removed from the other students, so that they will not overhear the testing.

The test items use several typefaces.

- **This red type indicates what you say.**
- This light type indicates what you do.
- *This italic type shows the student's answers.*

Some test items require you to point to the large letters that appear in this book. For these items, hold the book so that the student can see the letters.

The score sheet appears in the next column. Make one copy of the score sheet for each student. To use the score sheet, simply circle 1 point or 2 points if the student answers correctly.

SCORE SHEET

PART 1			PART 2		
Item	**Points**		**Item**	**Points**	
1b	0	1	1a	0	2
1c	0	1	1b	0	2
2b	0	1	2b	0	1
	0	1		0	1
	0	1	2c	0	1
	0	1		0	1
	0	1	2d	0	1
2d	0	1		0	1
	0	1	*Subtotal*	☐	
	0	1			
	0	1			
	0	1			
3b	0	2			
3c	0	2			
4b	0	2			
4d	0	2			
Subtotal	☐		**Total**	☐	

PLACEMENT TEST

PART 1

Task 1   Total possible: 2 points

(Circle 1 point on the scoring sheet for each correct response at *b* and *c*.)

This is an oral task. For step *c*, say the sound **d**, not the letter name.
a. You're going to say some sounds.
b. (test item) Say (pause) **rrr.** *rrr.*
c. (test item) Now say (pause) **d.** *d.*

Task 2   Total possible: 10 points

(Circle 1 point on the scoring sheet for each correct response at *b*.)

a. Point to the sounds. These are sounds.
Point to the boxed **m.** This sound is (pause)
mmm. What sound? Touch **m.** *mmm.*
b. (test items) Point to each unboxed sound in
the column. For each sound, ask: Is this
(pause) **mmm?**

(Circle 1 point on the scoring sheet for each correct response at step *d*.)

c. Point to the boxed **a.** This sound is (pause)
ăăă. What sound? Touch **a.** *ăăă.*
d. (test items) Point to each unboxed sound in
the column. For each sound, ask: Is this
(pause) **ăăă?**

Task 3 Total possible: 4 points

(Circle 2 points on the scoring sheet for each correct response at *b* and *c*.)

a. Let's play Say It Fast. Listen. **Ice** (pause) **box.** I can say it fast. **Icebox.**
b. (**test item**) Listen. **Foot** (pause) **ball.** (Pause.) Say it fast. *Football.* Yes, **football.**
c. (**test item**) Here's another word. (Pause.) **Nnnōōōzzz.** (Pause.) Say it fast. *Nose.* Yes, **nose.**

Task 4 Total possible: 4 points

(Circle 2 points on the scoring sheet for each correct response at *b* and *d*.)

This is an oral task. Do not stop between the sounds when saying zzzoooooo or wwwēēē.

a. First I'll say a word slowly. Then you'll say that word slowly. I'll say (pause) **zoo** slowly. Listen. (Pause.) **Zzzoooooo.**
b. (**test item**) Your turn. Say (pause) **zzzoooooo.** *Zzzoooooo.*
   (A child scores 2 points if he or she says the correct sounds without stopping between the sounds.)
c. Now I'll say (pause) **wē** slowly. Listen. (Pause.) **Wwwēēē.**
d. (**test item**) Your turn. Say (pause) **wwwēēē.**
   (A child scores 2 points if he or she says the correct sounds without stopping between the sounds.)

Add the number of points the child earned on part 1. Note: Administer part 2 **only** to children who made 19 or 20 points on part 1.

PART 2

Task 1 Total possible: 4 points

(Circle 2 points on the scoring sheet for each correct response at *a* and *b*.)

a. (**test item**) Point to the boxed **m.** Let's see if you remember this sound. (Pause.) What sound? Touch **m.** *mmm.*
b. (**test item**) Point to the boxed **a.** Let's see if you remember this sound. (Pause.) What sound? Touch **a.** *ăăă.*

Task 2 Total possible: 6 points

(Circle 1 point on the scoring sheet for each correct response at *b*, *c*, and *d*.)

a. I'll say a word slowly. Then I'll say it fast. Listen. (Pause.) **Mmmaaannn.** (Pause.) I can say it fast. **Man.**
b. (**test item**) Your turn. Say (pause) **iiinnn.** *iiinnn.*
   (**test item**) Say it fast. *In.*
c. (**test item**) Your turn. Say (pause) **aaat.** *Aaat.*
   (**test item**) Say it fast. *At.*
d. (**test item**) Your turn. Say (pause) **sssiiit.** *Sssiiit.*
   (**test item**) Say it fast. *Sit.*

End of Placement Test

Placement Guidelines

Part 1 of the Placement Test

Children who made 0–14 points begin with Reading Mastery I, lesson 1.

Children who made 15–18 points begin with Reading Mastery I, lesson 11.

Children who made 19–20 points should proceed with Part 2 of the placement test.

Part 2 of the Placement Test

Children who made 0–7 points begin with Reading Mastery I, lesson 11.

Children who made 8–10 points should be placed, if possible, in Reading Mastery: Fast Cycle I.

Reading Mastery II *and Fast cycle II*

For the *Reading Mastery II* placement test, each student reads a story aloud, as you count the student's decoding errors.

You will need to make one copy of the story on page 57. You should administer the test in a place that is somewhat removed from the other students, so that they will not overhear the testing.

Use the following procedures to administer the placement test.

1. Give the student a copy of the story.
2. Point to the passage and say, "I want you to read this story out loud. Take your time. Start with the title and read the story as well as you can."
3. Time the student and make one tally mark for each error. Use the following guidelines when tallying errors.
   - If the student misreads a word, tell the student the word and mark one error.
   - If the student reads a word incorrectly and then correctly, mark one error.
   - If the student sounds out a word instead of reading it normally, mark one error.
     (Note: Correct the student the first time the student sounds out a word. Ask the student, "What word is that?" If the student reads the word correctly, do not mark an error. If the student sounds out the word, mark an error. Do not correct the student on any subsequent sounding-outs.)
   - If the student does not identify a word within four seconds, tell the student the word and mark one error.
   - If the student skips a word, point to the word. If the student does not read the word correctly, mark one error.
   - If the student skips a line, point to the line. If the student does not read the line correctly, mark one error.
4. After two and a half minutes, stop the student. Count every word not read as an error. For example, if the student is eight words from the end of the passage at the end of the time limit, count eight errors.
5. Total the student's errors.

Placement Guidelines

Place your students as follows:

- Students who made 0 to 3 errors should be placed in lesson 11 of *Reading Mastery II*.
- Students who made 4 to 8 errors should be placed in lesson 1 of *Reading Mastery II*.
- Students who made more than 8 errors should be placed in *Reading Mastery I*. To determine an appropriate placement for these students, give them the individual rate-and-accuracy checkouts from *Reading Mastery I*. Start with the checkout for lesson 140. If the student passes this checkout, place the student in lesson 141. If the student does not pass this checkout, present the checkout for lesson 130. Continue working backward until the student passes a checkout. Place the student in the lesson that follows the checkout lesson.

the cow on the rōad

lots of men went down the rōad in a littlₑ car.

a cow was sitti͡ng on the rōad. sō the men ran to the cow. "wē will lift this cow," they said.

but the men did not lift the cow. "this cow is sō fat wē can not lift it."

the cow said, "I am not sō fat. I can lift mē." then the cow got in the car.

the men said, "now wē can not get in the car." sō the men sat on the rōad and the cow went hōmₑ in the car.

the end

III
see pg 61
for test

Reading Mastery III, IV, V and VI

The placement tests for *Reading Mastery III, IV, V, and VI* are similar in many respects. In part 1 of each test, individual students read a passage aloud as you count decoding errors. You will need to make one copy of the appropriate test for each student. You should administer part 1 in a place that is somewhat removed from the other students, so that they will not overhear the testing.

Use the following guidelines when counting decoding errors on part 1.

- If the student misreads a word, count one error.
- If the student omits a word ending, such as *s* or *ed*, count one error.
- If the student reads a word incorrectly and then correctly, count one error.
- If the student sounds out a word instead of reading it normally, count one error.
- If the student does not identify a word within three seconds, tell the student the word and count one error.
- If the student skips a word, count one error.
- If the student skips a line, point to the line and count one error.
- If the student does not finish the passage within the given time limit, count every word not read as an error. For example, if the student is eight words from the end of the passage at the end of the time limit, count eight errors.

Reading Mastery III

Instructions for Part 1

Use the following procedures to administer part 1.

1. Give the student a copy of the test on page 61.
2. Point to the passage and say, "You're going to read this passage out loud. I want you to read it as well as you can. Don't try to read it so fast that you make mistakes. But don't read it so slowly that it doesn't make any sense. You have one and a half minutes to read the passage. Go."
3. Time the student and make one tally mark for each error the student makes in the last thirteen lines of the passage, which are preceded by asterisks. (The first four lines serve as a "warm-up," so errors in the first four lines don't count.)

4. After one and a half minutes, stop the student. Count every word not read as an error.
5. Total the student's errors.

Instructions for Part 2

After all the students have finished part 1, administer part 2 to those students who made no more than four errors on part 1. Use the following procedures.

1. Assemble the students.
2. Give each student a copy of the test, and make sure the students have pencils.
3. Say, "Here is the passage that you read earlier. Follow along as I read the passage out loud. After I'm finished, you will write the answers to the questions in part 2."
4. Read the passage to the students.
5. Say, "Now write the answers to the questions in part 2. You have four minutes. Go."
6. Collect the tests after four minutes.
7. Total each student's errors, using the Answer Key.

Answer Key for Part 2

1. The elf
2. Red food is good to eat.
3. *Idea*: Because she was hungry
4. *Ideas*: All around; on the ground; on the side of the mountain
5. Just after Jean said, "But what and when."

Placement Guidelines

Place your students as follows:

- Students who made 0 or 1 **total** errors should be given the placement test for *Reading Mastery IV*.
- Students who made 0 to 3 errors on part 1 **and** 0 to 1 errors on part 2 should be placed in lesson 1 of *Reading Mastery III*.
- Students who made 4 to 7 errors on part 1 **and** 0 to 2 errors on part 2 should be placed in lesson A of *Reading Mastery III*.
- Students who made more than 8 errors on part 1 **or** more than 3 errors on part 2 should be given the placement test for *Reading Mastery II*.

Reading Mastery IV *See pg 62*

Instructions for Part 1

Use the following procedures to administer part 1.

1. Give the student a copy of the test on page 62.
2. Point to the column of words at the top of part 1.
3. Say, "Touch word 1." (Wait.) "That word is **California**."
4. Repeat step 3 for words 2-5.
5. Point to the passage and say, "You're going to read this passage out loud. I want you to read it as well as you can. Don't try to read it so fast that you make mistakes. But don't read it so slowly that it doesn't make any sense. You have two minutes to read the passage. Go."
6. Time the student and make one tally mark for each error.
7. After two minutes, stop the student. Count every word not read as an error.
8. Total the student's errors.

Instructions for Part 2.

After all the students have finished part 1, administer part 2 to those students who made no more than six errors on part 1. Use the following procedures.

1. Assemble the students.
2. Give each student a copy of the test, and make sure the students have pencils.
3. Say, "Here is the passage that you read earlier. Read the passage again silently; then answer the questions in part 2. You have five minutes. Go."
4. Collect the tests after five minutes.
5. Total each student's errors, using the Answer Key.

Answer Key for Part 2

1. *Idea*: Because the ship was on fire
2. *Idea*: Linda, Kathy
3. lifeboats
4. Linda
5. 13
6. 10
7. hand
8. *Idea*: In a lifeboat
9. Japan
10. *Idea*: To see their father
11. 3 days

Placement Guidelines

Place your students as follows:

- Students who made 0 or 1 **total** errors should be given the placement test for *Reading Mastery V*.
- Students who made 0 to 6 errors on part 1 **and** 0 to 2 errors on part 2 should be placed in *Reading Mastery IV*.
- Students who made more than 6 errors on part 1 **or** more than 2 errors on part 2 should be given the placement test for *Reading Mastery III*.

Reading Mastery V *pg 63*

Instructions for part 1

Use the following procedures to administer part 1.

1. Give the student a copy of the test on page 63.
2. Point to the passage and say, "You're going to read this passage out loud. I want you to read it as well as you can. Don't try to read it so fast that you make mistakes. But don't read it so slowly that it doesn't make any sense. You have two minutes to read the passage. Go."
3. Time the student and make one tally mark for each error.
4. After two minutes, stop the student. Count every word not read as an error.
5. Total the student's errors.

Instructions for Part 2.

After all the students have finished part 1, administer part 2 to the entire group. Use the following procedures.

1. Assemble the students.
2. Give each student a copy of the test, and make sure the students have pencils.
3. Say, "Here is the passage that you read earlier. Read the passage again silently; then answer the questions in part 2. You have seven minutes. Go."
4. Collect the tests after seven minutes.
5. Total each student's errors, using the Answer Key.

Answer Key for Part 2

1. *Idea*: The Bermuda Islands
2. *Ideas*: To dive; to see the bottom of the ocean
3. Warm
4. The guide
5. *Ideas*: partner; person
6. *Idea*: Signal the guide
7. *Idea*: Go to the surface
8. *Idea*: Get the bends
9. pressure

Placement Guidelines

Place your students as follows:

• Students who made 0 or 1 **total** errors should be given the placement test for *Reading Mastery VI*.

• Students who made 0 to 6 errors on part 1 **and** 0 to 2 errors on part 2 should be placed in *Reading Mastery V*.

• Students who made more than 6 errors on part 1 **or** more than 2 errors on part 2 should be given the placement test for *Reading Mastery IV*.

Reading Mastery VI

Instructions for Part 1

Use the following procedures to administer part 1.

1. Give the student a copy of the test on page 64.
2. Point to the passage and say, "You're going to read this passage out loud. I want you to read it as well as you can. Don't try to read it so fast that you make mistakes. But don't read it so slowly that it doesn't make any sense. You have two minutes to read the passage. Go."
3. Time the student and make one tally mark for each error.
4. After two minutes, stop the student. Count every word not read as an error.
5. Total the student's errors.

Instructions for Part 2

After all the students have finished part 1, administer part 2 to the entire group. Use the following procedures.

1. Assemble the students.
2. Give each student a copy of the test, and make sure the students have pencils.
3. Say, "Here is the passage that you read earlier. Read the passage again silently; then answer the questions in part 2. You have seven minutes. Go."
4. Collect the tests after seven minutes.
5. Total each student's errors, using the Answer Key.

Answer Key for Part 2

1. King
2. princess
3. *Ideas*: His daughter; Marygold
4. Gold
5. *Idea*: His daughter/gold
6. *Idea*: Because they weren't gold
7. Roses
8. perfume
9. *Idea*: The chink of one coin against another

Placement Guidelines

Place your students as follows:

• Students who made 0 to 6 errors on part 1 **and** 0 to 2 errors on part 2 should be placed in *Reading Mastery VI*.

• Students who made more than 6 errors on part 1 **or** more than 2 errors on part 2 should be given the placement test for *Reading Mastery V*.

PART 1

Jean was walking in a strange place. She was
close to mountains. And she was very hungry. She
said, "I wish I had something to eat."

Just then a strange little elf appeared. He said,
* "There is lots of food around here. You may eat all
* you want, but remember this rule: Red food is good to
* eat. See if you can say that rule."
* Jean said, "Red food is good to eat."
* The elf said, "Good remembering."
* Jean said, "I will remember that rule. But what
* and when . . ."
* The elf was suddenly gone. Jean said to herself,
* "That is strange. Just after I said 'But what and
* when,' the elf went away."
* Jean looked around and found lots of food. There
* was food on the ground. There was food on the side of
* the mountain.

PART 2

1. Who told the rule about red food? _____

2. What is the rule about red food? _____

_____

3. Why did Jean want something to eat?_____

_____

4. Where did Jean see food? _____

5. *Circle the answer.* When did the elf go away?

   ● Just after Jean said, "Here and there."

   ● Just after Jean said, "But what and when."

   ● After Jean ate.

Name _____

PART 1

1. California
2. Pacific
3. loudspeaker
4. lifeboat
5. Japan

● ● ● ● ● ● ● ●

"Fire! Fire!" a voice said over the loudspeaker. "The forward deck is on fire," the voice announced. "Everybody, leave the ship. Get into the lifeboats!"

Linda and her sister were on their way from the United States to Japan. Linda was thirteen years old, three years older than Kathy. Their father was in Japan, and they were on their way to visit him. Three days before, they had left California on a great ship called an ocean liner. They were now somewhere in the middle of the Pacific Ocean.

"Fire! Fire!" the voice shouted. "Everybody get into the lifeboats!"

People were running this way and that way on the deck of the ship. They were yelling and crying.

"Hold on to my hand," Linda said. The girls went to the lifeboats. People were all around them, shoving and yelling. Linda could not see much. She was afraid. Suddenly she was no longer holding Kathy's hand.

Suddenly a strong pair of arms grabbed Linda. "In you go," a voice said. A big man picked Linda up and put her in the lifeboat.

"Where's my sister?" Linda asked. Linda looked but she couldn't see her younger sister.

PART 2

1. Why was everybody trying to leave the ship? _____

_____

2. Name the two sisters that were on the ship. _____

3. People were trying to get into the

_____ .

4. Which sister was older? _____

5. How old was that girl? _____

6. How old was her sister? _____

7. Linda told Kathy, "Hold on to my

_____ ."

8. When the big man picked up Linda, where did he put her?

_____

9. What country were the girls going

to? _____

10. Why were the girls going there?

_____

_____

11. How long had they been on the

ship? _____

PART 1

An Underwater World

The diving boat was anchored in a place where the water changed from light green to dark, dark blue. One by one, the divers went down the ladder on the side of the boat and entered the warm water. The boat was about 1,600 kilometers east of Florida. They were south of the Bermuda Islands. Darla was the last diver to go down the ladder and enter the warm water.

"Now stick together," the guide said as he floated with his mask tilted back on his forehead. "You've got your partners. Stay with your partner. If you see something you want to look at, signal me. If one person stops, we all stop or somebody's going to get lost."

The guide continued, "If you get separated, go to the surface of the water. Don't try to look for the rest of us. Just go to the surface. And remember, don't go up too fast. Take at least two minutes to go up, or you may get the bends."

The bends. Darla had read about the bends. She knew that a person gets them because of the great pressure of the water.

PART 2

1. Near which islands does this story take place? _____

2. Why was the group in this place?

   _____

3. Was the water warm or cold?

   _____

4. Who led the group?

   _____

5. Each diver was supposed to stay with a

   _____.

6. What was a diver supposed to do if the diver wanted to stop and examine something?

   _____

7. What was a diver supposed to do if the diver got separated from the group?

   _____

8. What problem would the diver have if the diver went up to the surface too fast?

   _____

9. This problem was caused by the great

   _____ of the water.

PART 1

The Golden Touch

Once upon a time there lived a very rich king named Midas, who had a daughter named Marygold.

King Midas was very fond of gold. The only thing he loved more was his daughter. But the more Midas loved his daughter, the more he desired gold. He thought that the best thing he could possibly do for his child would be to give her the largest pile of yellow, glistening coins that had ever been heaped together since the world began. So, Midas gave all his thoughts and all his time to collecting gold. When he gazed at the gold-tinted clouds of sunset, he wished that they were real gold, and that they could be herded into his strong box. When little Marygold ran to meet him with a bunch of buttercups and dandelions, he used to say, "Pooh, pooh, child. If these flowers were as golden as they look, they would be worth picking."

And yet, in his earlier days, before he had this insane desire for gold, King Midas had shown a great love for flowers. He had planted a garden where there were the biggest and sweetest roses that any person ever saw or smelled. These roses were still growing in the garden, as large, as lovely, and as fragrant as they were when Midas used to pass whole hours looking at them, and inhaling their perfume. But now, if he looked at the flowers at all, it was only to calculate how much the garden would be worth if each of the rose petals were a thin plate of gold. And though he once was fond of music, the only music for poor Midas now was the chink of one coin against another.

PART 2

1. *Circle the answer.* What kind of royal person was Midas?

   ● Emperor   ● King   ● Prince

2. *Circle the answer.* So his daughter was _____.

   ● an empress   ● a queen   ● a princess

3. What did Midas love most of all?

   _____

4. What did he love almost as much?

   _____

5. But the more Midas loved _____,

   the more he desired _____.

6. Why didn't Midas think that dandelions were worth picking?

   _____

7. What kind of flowers had Midas planted in his earlier days?

   _____

8. Midas used to inhale the _____ of those flowers.

9. What was the only music that Midas loved now?

   _____

Sample Lessons

The following pages contain two sample lessons from *Reading Mastery* reproduced here in their entirety so that you can practice the skills discussed in this guide before presenting *Reading Mastery* to your students.

The first is lesson 108 from *Reading Mastery I*. The lesson begins with word reading activities in the *Presentation Book,* followed by the *Storybook* reading, and ending with various activities in the *Take-Home Book.*

The second sample lesson is lesson 77 from *Reading Mastery V.* The lesson begins with word reading activities in the *Presentation Book*, which includes the *Textbook* reading, and ending with various activities in the *Workbook* and *Skillbook.*

Lesson 108

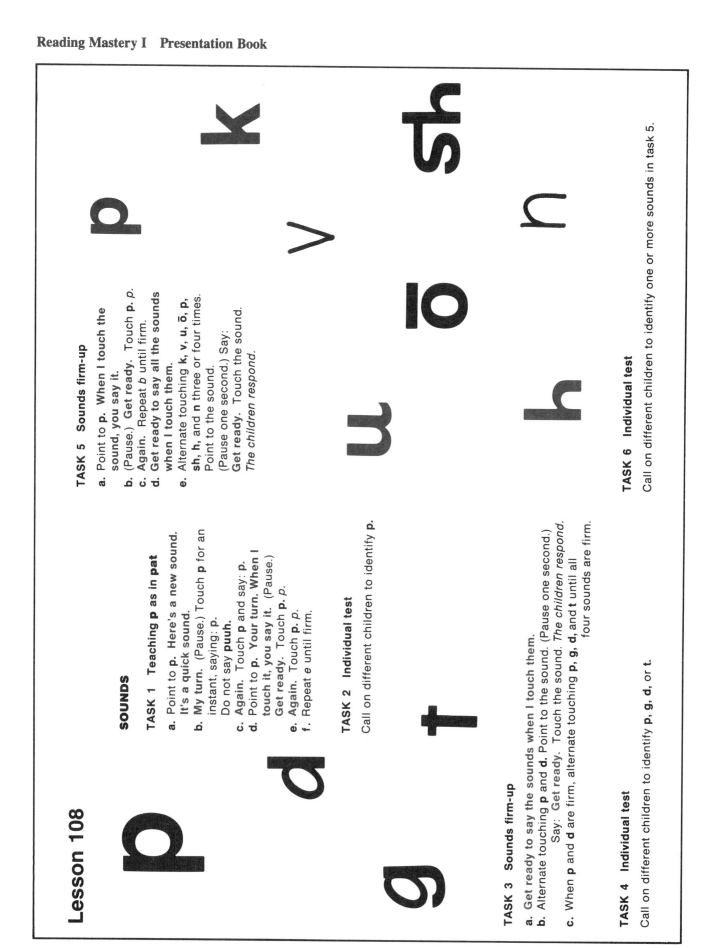

SOUNDS

TASK 1   Teaching p as in pat

a. Point to **p. Here's a new sound. It's a quick sound.**
b. **My turn.** (Pause.) Touch **p** for an instant, saying: **p.** Do not say **puuh.**
c. **Again.** Touch **p** and say: **p.**
d. Point to **p. Your turn. When I touch it, you say it.** (Pause.) Get ready. Touch **p. p.**
e. **Again.** Touch **p. p.**
f. Repeat **e** until firm.

TASK 2   Individual test

Call on different children to identify **p.**

TASK 3   Sounds firm-up

a. Get ready to say the sounds when I touch them.
b. Alternate touching **p** and **d.** Point to the sound. (Pause one second.) Say: Get ready. Touch the sound. *The children respond.*
c. When **p** and **d** are firm, alternate touching **p, g, d,** and **t** until all four sounds are firm.

TASK 4   Individual test

Call on different children to identify **p, g, d,** or **t.**

TASK 5   Sounds firm-up

a. Point to **p. When I touch the sound, you say it.**
b. (Pause.) Get ready. Touch **p. p.**
c. Again. Repeat **b** until firm.
d. Get ready to say all the sounds when I touch them.
e. Alternate touching **k, v, u, ō, p, sh, h,** and **n** three or four times. Point to the sound. (Pause one second.) Say: Get ready. Touch the sound. *The children respond.*

TASK 6   Individual test

Call on different children to identify one or more sounds in task 5.

108

READING VOCABULARY

TASK 7   Children rhyme with mop

a. Touch the ball for **mop**. You're going to read this word the
fast way. (Pause three seconds.) Get ready.
Move your finger quickly along the arrow. *Mop.*

b. Touch the ball for **cop**. This word rhymes with (pause) **mop.**
Move to **c**, then quickly along the arrow. *Cop.*
Yes, what word? (Signal.) *Cop.*

c. Touch the ball for **top**. This word rhymes with (pause) **mop.**
Move to **t**, then quickly along the arrow. *Top.*
Yes, what word? (Signal.) *Top.*

TASK 8   Children identify, then sound out an irregular word (was)

a. Touch the ball for **was**. Everybody, you're going to read this
word the fast way. (Pause three seconds.) Get ready.
Move your finger quickly along the arrow. *Was.* Yes, **was.**

b. Now you're going to sound out the word. Get ready.
Quickly touch **w**, **a**, **s** as the children say *wwwaaasss.*

c. Again.   Repeat *b.*
d. How do we say the word?   (Signal.) *Was.* Yes, **was.**
e. Repeat *b* and *d* until firm.

TASK 9   Individual test

Call on different children to do *b* and *d* in task 8.

TASK 10   Children read the fast way

Touch the ball for **ōld**. Get ready to read this word the fast way.
(Pause three seconds.) Get ready. (Signal.) *Old.*

TASK 11   Children read the words the fast way

Have the children read the words on this page the fast way.

TASK 12   Individual test

Call on different children to read one word the fast way.

mop

cop

top

was

ōld

108

TASK 13 Children identify, then sound out an irregular word (of)

a. Touch the ball for **of**. Everybody, you're going to read this word the fast way. (Pause three seconds.) **Get ready.** Move your finger quickly along the arrow. *Of.* **Yes, of.**

b. Now you're going to sound out the word. **Get ready.** Quickly touch **o**, **f** as the children say *ooofff*.

c. **Again.** Repeat *b*.
d. How do we say the word? (Signal.) *Of.* **Yes, of.**
e. Repeat *b* and *d* until firm.
f. Call on different children to do *b* and *d*.

TASK 14 Children identify, then sound out an irregular word (to)

Repeat the procedures in task 13 for **to**.

TASK 15 Children read the fast way

Touch the ball for **that**. Get ready to read this word the fast way. (Pause three seconds.) **Get ready.** (Signal.) *That.*

TASK 16 Children sound out the word and tell what word

a. Touch the ball for **cōat**. Sound it out.
b. **Get ready.** Touch **c**, **ō**, **t** as the children say *cōōōt*. If sounding out is not firm, repeat *b*.

c. What word? (Signal.) *Coat.* **Yes, coat.**

TASK 17 Children sound out the word and tell what word

a. Touch the ball for **gōat**. Sound it out.
b. **Get ready.** Touch **g**, **ō**, **t** as the children say *gōōōt*. If sounding out is not firm, repeat *b*.

c. What word? (Signal.) *Goat.* **Yes, goat.**

TASK 18 Children read the words the fast way

Have the children read the words on this page the fast way.

TASK 19 Individual test

Call on different children to read one word the fast way.

Do not touch any small letters.

of

to

that

cōat

gōat

Story 108

TASK 20   First reading—children read the story the fast way

Have the children reread any sentences containing words that give them trouble. Keep a list of these words.

a. Pass out Storybook 1.
b. Open your book to page 37 and get ready to read.
c. We're going to read this story the fast way.
d. Touch the first word. Check children's responses.
e. Reading the fast way. First word. (Pause three seconds.)
Get ready. Clap. *The.*
f. Next word. Check children's responses. (Pause three seconds.)
Get ready. Clap. *Old.*
g. Repeat f for the remaining words in the first sentence. Pause at least three seconds between claps. The children are to identify each word without sounding it out.
h. Repeat d through g for the next two sentences. Have the children reread the first three sentences until firm.
i. The children are to read the remainder of the story the fast way, stopping at the end of each sentence.
j. After the first reading of the story, print on the board the words that the children missed more than one time. Have the children sound out each word one time and tell what word.
k. After the group's responses are firm, call on individual children to read the words.

TASK 21   Individual test

a. I'm going to call on different children to read a whole sentence the fast way.
b. Call on different children to read a sentence. Do not clap for each word.

TASK 22   Second reading—children read the story the fast way and answer questions

a. You're going to read the story again the fast way and I'll ask questions.
b. First word. Check children's responses. Get ready. Clap. *The.*
c. Clap for each remaining word. Pause at least three seconds between claps. Pause longer before words that gave the children trouble during the first reading.
d. Ask the comprehension questions below as the children read.

After the children read:	You ask:
The old goat had an old coat.	**What did she have?** (Signal.) *An old coat.*
The old goat said, "I will eat this old coat."	**What did she say?** (Signal.) *I will eat this old coat.*
So she did.	**What did she do?** (Signal.) *She ate the old coat.*
"That was fun," she said.	**What did she say?** (Signal.) *That was fun.*
"I ate the old coat."	**What did the goat say?** (Signal.) *I ate the old coat.*
"And now I am cold."	**What did she say?** (Signal.) *And now I am cold.*
Now the old goat is sad.	**How does she feel?** (Signal.) *Sad.* **Why?** (Signal.) *The children respond.*

TASK 23   Picture comprehension

a. What do you think you'll see in the picture? *The children respond.*
b. Turn the page and look at the picture.
c. Ask these questions:
1. How does that goat feel? *The children respond.* Cold and sad.
2. Why is she out in the cold without a coat? *The children respond.* Because she ate her coat.
3. Did you ever go outside without a coat when it was cold? *The children respond.*

Take-Home 108

SUMMARY OF INDEPENDENT ACTIVITY

TASK 24   Introduction to independent activity

a. Pass out Take-Home 108 to each child.
b. Everybody, you're going to do this take-home on your own.
   Tell the children when they will work the items.
   Let's go over the things you're going to do.

TASK 25   Sentence copying

a. Hold up side 1 of your take-home and point to the first line in the
   sentence-copying exercise.
b. Everybody, here's the sentence you're going to write on the lines
   below.
c. Get ready to read the words in this sentence the fast way.
   First word. Check children's responses. Get ready. Clap. *Thē.*
d. Next word. Check children's responses. Get ready. Clap. *Goat.*
e. Repeat *d* for the remaining words.
f. After you finish your take-home, you get to draw a picture about
   the sentence, **thē gōat āte thē cōat.**

TASK 26   Sound writing

a. Point to the sound-writing exercise. Here are the sounds you're
   going to write today. I'll touch the sounds. You say them.
b. Touch each sound. *The children respond.*
c. Repeat the series until firm.

TASK 27   Matching

a. Point to the column of words in the Matching Game.
b. Everybody, you're going to follow the lines and write these words.
c. Reading the fast way.
d. Point to the first word. (Pause.) Get ready. (Signal.)
   The children respond.
e. Repeat *d* for the remaining words.
f. Repeat *d* and *e* until firm.

TASK 28   Cross-out game

Point to the boxed word in the Cross-out Game. Everybody, here's
the word you're going to cross out today. What word? (Signal.)
Not. Yes, **not.**

TASK 29   Pair relations

a. Point to the pair-relations exercise on side 2. You're going to circle
   the picture in each box that shows what the words say.
b. Point to the space at the top of the page. After you finish,
   remember to draw a picture that shows **thē gōat āte thē cōat.**

TASK 30   2½-minute individual checkout

Make a permanent chart for recording results of individual checkouts.
See Teacher's Guide for sample chart.

a. As you are doing your take-home, I'll call on children one at a time
   to read the **whole story.** If you can read the whole story the fast
   way in less than two and a half minutes and if you make no more
   than three errors, I'll put two stars after your name on the chart for
   lesson 108.
b. If you make too many errors or don't read the story in less than
   two and a half minutes, you'll have to practice it and do it again.
   When you do read it in under two and a half minutes with no more
   than three errors, you'll get one star. Remember, two stars if you
   can do it the first time, one star if you do it the second or third
   time you try.
c. Call on a child. Tell the child: Read the whole story very carefully
   the fast way. Go.   Time the child. If the child makes a mistake,
   quickly tell the child the correct word and permit the child to continue
   reading. As soon as the child makes more than three errors or
   exceeds the time limit, tell the child to stop. You'll have to read the
   story to yourself and try again later. Plan to monitor the child's
   practice.
d. Record two stars for each child who reads appropriately.
   Congratulate those children.
e. Give children who do not earn two stars a chance to read the story
   again before the next lesson is presented. Award one star to each of
   those children who meet the rate and accuracy criterion.

END OF LESSON 108

STORY 108

STORY 108

thē ōld gōₐt had an ōld cōₐt.

thē ōld gōₐt said, "I will ēₐt this

ōld cōₐt." sō shē did.

"that was fun," shē said. "I ātₑ

thē ōld cōₐt. and now I am cōld."

now thē ōld gōₐt is sad.

TAKE-HOME 108 SIDE 2

tāil   hē   shē   māil

a rug   shacₖ   nōsₑ   hut

thē sacₖs   licₖ   a rākₖ   fēēt

NAME

TAKE-HOME 108 SIDE 1

thē gōₐt ātₑ thē cōₐt.

the goat ate the coat

g ___ hit

c ___ ōld

k ___ sāve

d ___ how

t ___ I

not

not   nōsₑ   not   fish   not   hē

sacₖ   not   now   not   that   not   not

not   got   not   hāt.   is

Lesson 77

Lesson 77

PART A   Word Lists

1	2	3
linen	precious	flexible
frenzy	delicious	convenient
appetite	anxious	inconvenient
credit	spacious	accompany
woven		accompanied
dispair		
pity		
secure		

4
Vocabulary words
1. deserve credit
2. linen
3. frenzy
4. occupied
5. envy
6. despair

5
Vocabulary words
1. discontent
2. appetite
3. secure
4. pity

PART B
Vocabulary Sentences

1. She was very unhappy about a lot of things, but she was most <u>discontented</u> about the mess that was in the basement.
2. When he started eating he had a huge <u>appetite</u>, but when he finished the main part of the meal, he had no room for dessert.
3. He didn't want anybody to steal his treasure, so he looked for a <u>secure</u> place.
4. The little boy was so poor, sad, and cold that I felt great <u>pity</u> for him.

WORD PRACTICE AND VOCABULARY

EXERCISE 1   Word practice

1. Everybody, find lesson 77, part A in your skillbook. *Wait.* Touch under each word in column 1 as I read it.
2. The first word is **linen.**
3. Next word. **Frenzy.**
4. *Repeat step 3 for each remaining word in column 1.*
5. Your turn. Read the first word. *Signal.* **Linen.**
6. Next word. *Signal.* **Frenzy.**
7. *Repeat step 6 for each remaining word in column 1.*
8. *Repeat the words in column 1 until firm.*

EXERCISE 2   Word family

1. Everybody, touch column 2. *Check.* All those words end with the letters **i-o-u-s.** Touch under the first word. *Pause.* What word? *Signal.* **Precious.**
2. Next word. *Pause.* What word? *Signal.* **Delicious.**
3. *Repeat step 2 for each remaining word in column 2.*
4. *Repeat the words in column 2 until firm.*

EXERCISE 3   Word practice

1. Everybody, touch under the first word in column 3. *Pause.* What word? *Signal.* **Flexible.**
2. Next word. *Pause.* What word? *Signal.* **Convenient.**
3. *Repeat step 2 for each remaining word in column 3.*
4. *Repeat the words in column 3 until firm.*

EXERCISE 4   Vocabulary development

Task A
1. Everybody, touch column 4. *Check.* First you're going to read the words in column 4. Then we'll talk about what they mean.

2. Touch under the first line. *Pause.* What words? *Signal.* **Deserve credit.**
3. Next word. *Pause.* What word? *Signal.* **Linen.**
4. *Repeat step 3 for each remaining word in column 4.*
5. *Repeat the words in column 4 until firm.*

Task B
1. Now let's talk about what those words mean. The words in line 1 are **deserve credit.** When you succeed in doing something, you **deserved credit** for doing that thing. Here's another way of saying **She succeeded at solving the problem: She deserved credit for solving the problem.** Everybody, what's another way of saying **She succeeded at solving the problem?** *Signal.* **She deserved credit for solving the problem.**
2. Everybody, what's another way of saying **She succeeded at having good manners?** *Signal.* **She deserved credit for having good manners.**

Task C
Word 2 is **linen. Linen** is an expensive cloth that some sheets and dresses are made of. Everybody, what's an expensive cloth that some sheets and dresses are made of? *Signal.* **Linen.**

Task D
1. Word 3 is **frenzy.** When you do things in a very hurried and excited way, you do them in a **frenzy.** Here's another way of saying **She ran around in excitement: She ran around in a frenzy?** Everybody, what's another way of saying **She ran around in excitement?** *Signal.* **She ran around in a frenzy.**
2. Everybody, what's another way of saying **They cooked the dinner in a hurry?** *Signal.* **They cooked the dinner in a frenzy.**

Task E
1. Word 4 is **occupied.** When you are **occupied** with something, you are busy with that thing. Here's another way of saying **You are busy with your thoughts: You are occupied with your thoughts.**
2. Everybody, what's another way of saying **She was busy with the customer?** *Signal.* **She was occupied with the customer.**
3. Everybody, what's another way of saying **They were busy with the details of the problem?** *Signal.* **They were occupied with the details of the problem.**

Task F

Word 5 is **envy.** When you **envy** people, you wish you could do something that they can do. If you wish you had somebody's wealth, you envy that person for his wealth. If you wish you had a person's skill, you envy that person for her skill.

Task G

Word 6 is **despair.** When you feel no hope, you feel **despair.**

EXERCISE 5   Vocabulary from context

Task A

1. Everybody, touch column 5. *Check.* First you're going to read the words in column 5. Then we'll talk about what they mean.
2. Touch under the first word. *Pause.* What word? *Signal.* **Discontent.**
3. Next word. *Pause.* What word? *Signal.* **Appetite.**
4. *Repeat step 3 for each remaining word in column 5.*
5. *Repeat the words in column 5 until firm.*

Task B

1. Everybody, find part B in your skillbook. *Check.* I'll read those sentences. You figure out what the underlined part in each sentence means.
2. Sentence one. She was very unhappy about a lot of things, but she was most discontented about the mess that was in the basement. *Call on a student.* What could **discontented** mean? *Idea:* Dissatisfied.
3. *Repeat step 2 for each remaining sentence.* *Answer Key:* **2.** *Idea:* Desire for food.
   3. *Idea:* Safe.
   4. *Idea:* Sorrow.

STORY READING

EXERCISE 6   Decoding and comprehension

1. Everybody, turn to page 292 in your textbook. *Wait. Call on a student.* What's the error limit for this lesson? **6 errors.**
2. *Call on individual students to read. Present the tasks specified for each circled letter.*
Ⓐ Where was Midas at the end of the last part? *Idea:* In his treasure room.
● Who was with him? **A stranger.**
● What did Midas think this stranger was? **A god.**
● Why did Midas think this god had paid him a visit? *Idea:* To grant him a favor.
Ⓑ Did Midas think that he had enough gold? **No.**
Ⓒ If you think about the title of this story, you'll know what Midas will wish for. What is that? *Idea:* The golden touch.
● How would a golden touch work? *Idea:* Everything you touch turns into gold.
Ⓓ Is Midas thinking clearly? **No.**
● Name some problems that you might have if everything you touched turned into gold. *Response:* Student preference.
● Read the rest of the story to yourselves and be ready to answer some questions.
After all students have finished reading:
● When did the stranger say that Midas would have the golden touch? *Idea:* At sunrise the next morning.

Lesson 77

The Golden Touch
PART 2Ⓐ

The stranger gazed about the room, and when his glowing smile had shone upon all the golden objects that were there, he turned again to Midas.

"You are a wealthy man, friend Midas," he observed. "I doubt whether any other four walls on earth contain so much gold as this room contains."

"I have done pretty well—pretty well," answered Midas in a discontented tone. "But, after all, it is a very small amount, when you consider that it has taken me my whole life to get it together."Ⓑ Midas continued, "If one could live a thousand years, he might have time to grow rich."

"What?" exclaimed the stranger. "Then you are not satisfied?"

Midas shook his head.

"And what would satisfy you?" asked the stranger. "I would like to know."

Midas paused. He felt that this stranger had the power to grant any wish. He had only to speak and obtain whatever he might want. So he thought, and thought, and thought. His imagination heaped up one golden mountain after another. But he was unable to imagine mountains that were big enough. At last, a bright idea occurred to King Midas. It seemed

really as bright as the glistening metal which he loved so much.

Raising his head, he looked the stranger in the face.

The visitor observed, "Well, Midas, I see that you have at last hit upon something that will satisfy you. Tell me your wish."Ⓒ

"It is only this," replied Midas. "I am weary of collecting my treasures with so much trouble, and seeing the heap so small after I have done my best. I wish everything that I touch could be changed to gold!"

"The Golden Touch!" exclaimed the stranger. "You certainly deserve credit, friend Midas, for having such a brilliant idea. But are you quite sure that this will satisfy you?"

"How could it fail?" said Midas.

"And you will never regret having it?"

"What could make me regret it?" asked Midas. "I need nothing else to make me perfectly happy."Ⓓ ★6 ERRORS★

"You shall have your wish," replied the stranger, waving his hand in farewell. "Tomorrow, at sunrise, you will find yourself gifted with the Golden Touch."

The stranger then became so terribly

bright that Midas closed his eyes. When he opened them again he saw only one yellow sunbeam in the room. All around him was the glistening of the precious metal which he had spent his life collecting.

Midas did not sleep well that night. His mind was like the mind of a child who had been promised a new plaything in the morning. Day had hardly peeped over the hills when King Midas was wide awake. He stretched his arms out of bed and began to touch objects that were within reach. He was anxious to prove whether the Golden Touch had really come, according to the stranger's promise.

Midas laid his finger on a chair by the bedside, and on other things, but he was very disappointed to find that they remained exactly the same as before. He was afraid that he had only dreamed about the stranger, or else that the stranger had been making fun of him. And how miserable it would be if Midas had to be content with the little gold he could scrape together by ordinary means, instead of creating gold by a touch.

All this happened while it was only the gray of the morning, with only a streak of brightness along the edge of the sky. Midas was in a very bad mood. He kept growing sadder and sadder, until the earliest sunbeam shone through the window and lit up the ceiling over his head. It seemed to Midas that this bright yellow sunbeam reflected in an unusual way on the white covering of the bed. Looking more closely, he was astonished and delighted to find that this linen cloth had been changed into

woven gold, the purest and brightest he had ever seen! The Golden Touch had come to him with the first sunbeam!

Midas started up in a kind of joyful frenzy, and ran about the room grasping at everything that happened to be in his way. He seized one of the bedposts, and it immediately became a golden pillar. He pulled open a window curtain, and the cord grew heavy in his hand—a mass of gold. Midas took up a book from the table. At his first touch, the cover became solid gold. And when he ran his fingers through the pages, the book became a bundle of thin, gold plates, and all the wise words in the book disappeared.

Midas quickly put on his clothes, and was overjoyed to see himself in a magnificent suit of gold cloth, which was flexible and soft, although it was very, very heavy. He drew out his handkerchief, which little Marygold had made for him. That was also gold.

Somehow or other this last change did not quite please King Midas. He would have rather had his little daughter's handkerchief remain just as it was when she climbed upon his knee and put it into his hand.

But it was not worthwhile to worry about a handkerchief. Midas now took his spectacles from his pocket and put them on his nose to see more clearly. But he discovered that he could not possibly see through them, for the glass had turned into a plate of yellow metal. They were worthless as spectacles, but valuable as gold. It seemed rather inconvenient to Midas that, with all

his wealth, he could never again be rich enough to own a pair of usable spectacles.

"It is no great problem," he said to himself. "Every great good is accompanied by some small inconvenience. The Golden Touch is worth the loss of a pair of spectacles. My own eyes will serve for ordinary purposes, and little Marygold will soon be old enough to read to me."

Wise King Midas was so excited by his good fortune that the palace did not seem large enough for him. He therefore went downstairs, and smiled when he observed that the handrail of the staircase became a bar of gold as his hand passed over it. He lifted the door latch. It was

brass only a moment ago, but it became golden when his fingers left it. He went into the garden, where he found a great number of beautiful roses in full bloom, and others in all the stages of lovely bud and blossom. Their fragrance was very delicious in the morning breeze.

But Midas knew a way to make them far more precious, to his way of thinking. So he went from bush to bush, and used his magic touch until every flower and bud was changed to gold. By the time this work was completed, King Midas was called to breakfast. The morning air had given him an excellent appetite, and he quickly returned to the palace.

- How well did Midas sleep that night? *Idea:* Not very well.
- Did Midas get up in the morning **before** sunrise or **after** sunrise? **Before sunrise.**
- When did Midas notice that he had the golden touch? *Idea:* When the first sunbeam came into his room.
- What was the first thing that had been changed into gold? *Idea:* The bed covering.
- What happened to the book that he touched? *Idea:* It turned into gold.
- What was lost when the book changed into gold? *Idea:* All the wise words.
- When Midas's clothes changed into gold, what else was different about them? *Idea:* They were heavier.
  Gold is very, very heavy.
- What was the first thing that Midas regretted turning into gold? *Idea:* His handkerchief.
- What was the problem with his spectacles? *Idea:* He couldn't see through them.
- How did Midas plan to solve the problem of not being able to see clearly? *Idea:* Have Marygold help him.
- What did he do in the garden? *Idea:* Turned all the roses into gold.
- Why did he return to the palace at the end of this part? *Idea:* He was called for breakfast.
- What do you think is going to happen when he tries to eat breakfast? *Response:* Student preference.

Award 4 points or have the students reread to the error limit sign.

INDEPENDENT WORK

Do all the items in your skillbook and workbook for lesson 77.

ANSWER KEY FOR WORKBOOK

Story Items

1. Put the following events in the right order by numbering them from 1 through 4.

    _3_ Midas turned a book to gold.

    _4_ Midas turned a rose to gold.

    _1_ Midas asked the stranger for a favor.

    _2_ Midas had a hard time sleeping.

Review Items

2. Write which god each picture shows. Choose from **Apollo, Hermes, Poseidon** or **Zeus.**

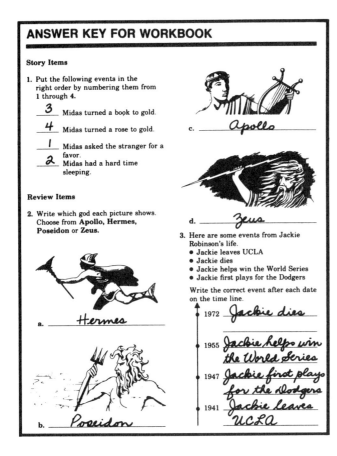

a. _Hermes_

b. _Poseidon_

c. _Apollo_

d. _Zeus_

3. Here are some events from Jackie Robinson's life.
    • Jackie leaves UCLA
    • Jackie dies
    • Jackie helps win the World Series
    • Jackie first plays for the Dodgers

    Write the correct event after each date on the time line.

    1972 _Jackie dies_

    1955 _Jackie helps win the World Series_

    1947 _Jackie first plays for the Dodgers_

    1941 _Jackie leaves UCLA_

WORKCHECK AND AWARDING POINTS

1. *Read the questions and answers for the skillbook and workbook.*

2. *Award points for independent work as follows:*

0 errors	6 points
2 errors	4 points
3, 4, or 5 errors	2 points
5 or more errors	0 points

3. *Award bonus points as follows:*

Correcting missed items or getting all items right	2 points
Doing the writing assignment acceptably	2 points

ANSWER KEY FOR SKILLBOOK

PART C

1. *Idea:* Baucis and Philemon were kind to strangers.

PART D

2. **a.** No
   b. *Idea:* It wouldn't have been enough
   c. *Idea:* The golden touch
   d. No

3. **a.** No
   b. *Idea:* At sunrise
   c. *Idea:* The bed covering
   d. *Idea:* Read it

4. **a.** *Idea:* They were heavier
   b. His handkerchief
   c. *Ideas:* Marygold; his daughter

5. **a.** Roses
   b. *Idea:* Good
   c. *Idea:* They had no smell

PART E

6. **a.** Greyhound
   b. Collie
   c. Hound
   d. Poodle
   e. Airedale

7. **a.** Lion
   b. Cat that Walked
   c. Lion
   d. Ugly Duckling
   e. Cat that Walked

8. **a.** disagreeable
   b. main job
   c. contract
   d. in disguise
   e. astonishment
   f. inhabitants
   g. spacious
   h. a lot of

Lesson 77

R IW B T

Story Items

1. Put the following events in the right order by numbering them from **1** through **4**.

   _____ Midas turned a book to gold.

   _____ Midas turned a rose to gold.

   _____ Midas asked the stranger for a favor.

   _____ Midas had a hard time sleeping.

Review Items

2. Write which god each picture shows. Choose from **Apollo, Hermes, Poseidon** or **Zeus.**

a. _____

b. _____

c. _____

d. _____

3. Here are some events from Jackie Robinson's life.
   - Jackie leaves UCLA
   - Jackie dies
   - Jackie helps win the World Series
   - Jackie first plays for the Dodgers

   Write the correct event after each date on the time line.

   1972 _____

   _____

   1955 _____

   _____

   1947 _____

   _____

   1941 _____

   _____

Lesson 77

PART A   Word Lists

1
linen
frenzy
appetite
credit
woven
dispair
pity
secure

2
precious
delicious
anxious
spacious

3
flexible
convenient
inconvenient
accompany
accompanied

4
Vocabulary words
1. deserve credit
2. linen
3. frenzy
4. occupied
5. envy
6. despair

5
Vocabulary words
1. discontent
2. appetite
3. secure
4. pity

PART B
Vocabulary Sentences

1. She was very unhappy about a lot of things, but she was most <u>discontented</u> about the mess that was in the basement.
2. When he started eating he had a huge <u>appetite</u>, but when he finished the main part of the meal, he had no room for dessert.
3. He didn't want anybody to steal his treasure, so he looked for a <u>secure</u> place.
4. The little boy was so poor, sad, and cold that I felt great <u>pity</u> for him.

PART C   Main Idea Paragraphs

Read the paragraph below. Then write a sentence that tells the main idea.

1.   Baucis and Philemon lived in a small cottage outside a village. They did not have much money or food, but they were happy. Sometimes, they would see a stranger walking up the path to their cottage. At those times, Baucis would hurry into the house to make dinner and Philemon would greet the stranger. Then Baucis and Philemon would give the stranger some dinner and do everything they could to make the stranger comfortable. After dinner, they would give up their bed to the stranger and sleep on the floor.

PART D   Story Items

2. a. Before the stranger came to his room, was Midas satisfied with the wealth he had?
   b. Why didn't Midas just ask for a mountain of gold?

   c. What did Midas ask the stranger for?
   d. Did Midas think he would ever regret that gift?
3. Midas woke up early the next morning.
   a. Did the golden touch work at first?
   b. When did the golden touch begin to work?
   c. What was the first object that changed into gold?
   d. After Midas touched the book, what couldn't he do with that book?
4. a. When Midas put on his clothes, what was different about their weight?
   b. Write the name of the first object that disturbed Midas when it changed to gold.
   c. Who had made that object for Midas?
5. a. What kind of flowers did Midas touch?
   b. How did the flowers smell before he touched them?
   c. How did they smell after he touched them?

PART E   Review Items

6. Write which breed of dog each statement describes.
   a. This is the fastest breed.
   b. This breed is good at herding.
   c. This breed has an excellent nose.
   d. This may be the smartest breed.
   e. This breed is very brave.

7. Write which character could have made each statement. Choose from the **Lion,** the **Cat that Walked,** or the **Ugly Duckling.**
   a. "I am the king of beasts."
   b. "I live with people, but they can't tell me what to do."
   c. "I used to be a coward."
   d. "I finally saw myself when I looked in the water."
   e. "I saw how the woman fooled all the other animals."

8. Use the words in the box to fill in the blanks or replace the underlined words.

disagreeable	insulted	rookie
astonishment	contract	beat
main job	a lot of	spacious
in disguise	inhabitants	

   a. The rainy weather was very _____ to Sidney.
   b. Cora decided to go to a school that would prepare her for a new <u>career</u>.
   c. She didn't want to perform in the play, but she had a _____ that said she had to.
   d. At the Halloween party, Mary was _____ as a bear.
   e. They were surprised and full of <u>amazement</u>.
   f. Most of the _____ of the town chased the frogs into the lake.
   g. Their footsteps echoed in the _____ halls.
   h. They loaded their sled with <u>abundant</u> supplies.

PART F   Writing Assignment

Write at least **four** sentences about the problems you might have if you had the golden touch.